AF782531

THE VETERANS' MAJOR MEDICAL FACILITIES CONSTRUCTION ACT OF 2002

WEDNESDAY, APRIL 24, 2002

HOUSE OF REPRESENTATIVES,
SUBCOMMITTEE ON HEALTH,
COMMITTEE ON VETERANS' AFFAIRS,
Washington, DC

The subcommittee met, pursuant to notice, at 3:25 p.m., in room 344, Cannon House Office Building, Hon. John Boozman (acting chairman of the subcommittee) presiding.

Present: Representatives Boozman, Moran, Filner, Berkley, Snyder, Brown, and Miller.

OPENING STATEMENT OF HON. JOHN BOOZMAN, ACTING CHAIRMAN

Mr. BOOZMAN. Good afternoon. The subcommittee will come to order.

I want to thank you all for being here today. I apologize for the delay. I'm a little out of breath. I've been running back and forth trying to let everybody be aware of what was going on.

Certainly, we've got a very important topic today, authorization of the VA Medical Facilities Construction for fiscal year 2003.

Capital improvement in VA health care is a matter of rising frustration to the committee, and worrisome for a number of VA facilities that are in need of repairs. Because of CARES and its slow pace, we have not seen many projects go forward in the past several years, and this situation needs resolution.

The bill before us, a bill introduced by Chairman Moran, with the ranking member, H.R. 4514, would authorize 10 major projects. These are among the VA's highest priorities for the year, and four of them are included in the President's budget for fiscal year 2003, so presumably, they are non-controversial.

We look forward to the VA's views on the remaining six projects our bill would authorize.

The House resolution on the budget includes sufficient funding to support appropriations for the 10 projects authorized by our bill, an amount of $285 billion in major construction appropriations.

Also, the bill would raise the minor to major dollar threshold from $4 million to $6 million, the first increase in 7 years, and would provide specific guidance to the VA Secretary on spending the higher minor construction appropriations it authorizes.

In accord with the committee's priority that funds be devoted not only to life, safety hazards, such as seismic protection, but also improve specialized medical programs such as mental health, spinal cord and brain injury facilities, and long-term care units such as VA nursing homes.

Our bill also addresses needs for VA to provide additional attention to its vital biomedical research programs. A number of VA research laboratories, and other facilities affecting our research are urgently in need of attention and improvement.

I want to thank Dr. Snyder for his influence and assistance in having the subcommittee address the issue of VA research facilities again with this bill as in H.R. 811 and in the first session of this Congress.

Dr. Snyder, would you like to comment?

Dr. SNYDER. I'll just make a comment that President Clinton may be gone, but Arkansas still controls the world here, very much so. (Laughter.)

Mr. BOOZMAN. Both he and I are from Arkansas, so Arkansas is well-represented here.

So let's get started with our hearing. Our first panel, Mr. Mark Catlett, principal deputy assistant secretary for management; accompanied by Mr. Robert Neary, assistant chief facilities management officer, Veterans' Health Administration; also Mr. Gary Rossio, chef executive of the VA San Diego Health Care System; Mr. Alex Spector, director, Alaska VA Health Care System and Regional Office; and Col. David Gilbreath, Commander, Elmendorf Air Force Base Hospital, Anchorage, Alaska.

We appreciate all of y'all being here today, especially the long-distance flyers from California and Alaska. I look forward to your advice on these matters.

I'd like to have the record reflect that with this Elmendorf project, local VA and DOD officials are working in concert on another matter of great importance to the committee, that of VA/DOD health resources sharing, so we really appreciate your coming today to discuss this joint project for a new medical facility.

Let's go ahead and get started, then. Mr. Catlett, and then Col. Gilbreath.

STATEMENTS OF D. MARK CATLETT, PRINCIPAL DEPUTY ASSISTANT SECRETARY FOR MANAGEMENT, DEPARTMENT OF VETERANS AFFAIRS, ACCOMPANIED BY ROBERT L. NEARY, ACTING ASSOCIATE CHIEF, STRATEGIC MANAGEMENT OFFICE; GARY ROSSIO, CHIEF EXECUTIVE OFFICER, VA SAN DIEGO HEALTH CARE SYSTEM; AND ALEX SPECTOR, DIRECTOR, ALASKA VA HEALTH CARE SYSTEM AND REGIONAL OFFICE; AND COL. DAVID D. GILBREATH, COMMANDER, ELMENDORF AIR FORCE BASE HOSPITAL

STATEMENT OF D. MARK CATLETT

Mr. CATLETT. Thank you, Mr. Chairman. It's a pleasure to be here on this panel before you.

I am pleased to testify today on behalf of the Department of Veterans Affairs regarding H.R. 4514, entitled the Veterans' Major Medical Facilities Construction Act of 2002, which authorizes the Secretary of Veterans Affairs to carry out certain major medical construction projects, as well as addressing other matters related to VA's construction program.

THE VETERANS' MAJOR MEDICAL FACILITIES CONSTRUCTION ACT OF 2002

HEARING

BEFORE THE

SUBCOMMITTEE ON HEALTH

OF THE

COMMITTEE ON VETERANS' AFFAIRS
HOUSE OF REPRESENTATIVES

ONE HUNDRED SEVENTH CONGRESS

SECOND SESSION

APRIL 24, 2002

Printed for the use of the Committee on Veterans' Affairs

Serial No. 107–27

U.S. GOVERNMENT PRINTING OFFICE

86–875PDF WASHINGTON : 2003

For sale by the Superintendent of Documents, U.S. Government Printing Office
Internet: bookstore.gpo.gov Phone: toll free (866) 512–1800; DC area (202) 512–1800
Fax: (202) 512–2250 Mail: Stop SSOP, Washington, DC 20402–0001

COMMITTEE ON VETERANS' AFFAIRS

CHRISTOPHER H. SMITH, New Jersey, *Chairman*

BOB STUMP, Arizona
MICHAEL BILIRAKIS, Florida
TERRY EVERETT, Alabama
STEVE BUYER, Indiana
JACK QUINN, New York
CLIFF STEARNS, Florida
JERRY MORAN, Kansas
HOWARD P. (BUCK) McKEON, California
JIM GIBBONS, Nevada
MICHAEL K. SIMPSON, Idaho
RICHARD H. BAKER, Louisiana
ROB SIMMONS, Connecticut
ANDER CRENSHAW, Florida
HENRY E. BROWN, Jr., South Carolina
JEFF MILLER, Florida
JOHN BOOZMAN, Arkansas

LANE EVANS, Illinois
BOB FILNER, California
LUIS V. GUTIERREZ, Illinois
CORRINE BROWN, Florida
JULIA CARSON, Indiana
SILVESTRE REYES, Texas
VIC SNYDER, Arkansas
CIRO D. RODRIGUEZ, Texas
RONNIE SHOWS, Mississippi
STEPHEN F. LYNCH, Massachusetts
SHELLEY BERKLEY, Nevada
BARON P. HILL, Indiana
TOM UDALL, New Mexico
SUSAN A. DAVIS, California

PATRICK E. RYAN, *Chief Counsel and Staff Director*

SUBCOMMITTEE ON HEALTH

JERRY MORAN, Kansas, *Chairman*

CLIFF STEARNS, Florida,
HOWARD P. (BUCK) McKEON, California
JIM GIBBONS, Nevada
MICHAEL K. SIMPSON, Idaho
RICHARD H. BAKER, Louisiana
ROB SIMMONS, Connecticut
ANDER CRENSHAW, Florida
HENRY E. BROWN, Jr., South Carolina
JEFF MILLER, Florida
JOHN BOOZMAN, Arkansas

BOB FILNER, California
RONNIE SHOWS, Mississippi
SHELLEY BERKLEY, Nevada
CIRO D. RODRIGUEZ, Texas
LUIS V. GUTIERREZ, Illinois
VIC SNYDER, Arkansas
STEPHEN F. LYNCH, Massachusetts

CONTENTS

April 24, 2002

Mr. Chairman, my comments regarding this bill will pertain to the four substantive sections, and let's get right to that.

In Section 2 of the bill, 4514, it would authorize the Secretary to carry out 10 major medical construction projects.

As you noted, four of those are seismic projects that are included in our budget, two at Palo Alto, one at San Francisco, and one at West L.A. They were included in the President's 2003 budget submission to the Congress.

The selection of these projects was the result of a thorough capital investment selection process in which specific needs of the VA were balanced against the Department's strategic goals within the parameters of annual budget and management constraints.

The ultimate result of this process was the selection of four major projects, as we've noted, that the VA believes best achieves the balance and that reflects a sound financial investment.

Moreover, the projects selected by the Department are the least likely to be affected by the ongoing CARES process, and I'm sure we'll talk about that some more as we go through this hearing.

As you know, the CARES process has been implemented to improve access and quality of veteran' health care through realigning VA's capital assets. CARES is an objective evidence-based evaluation of clinical services required in the year 2020 by market area.

While I am addressing the projects included in H.R. 4514, I would like to mention that our 2003 budget requested authorization for the lease of a satellite outpatient clinic in Charlotte, North Carolina, in the amount of $2.6 million. We would ask that this authorization be included in the bill when it is marked up.

Section 3 of the bill authorizes the appropriation sum of $285 million for the 2003 construction budget for these 10 major projects.

My comment on 3 is consistent with what we just covered for Section 2.

Specifically, it is that the VA's determination of only four projects listed in the budget should be carried out at this time. The amount authorized to be appropriated for fiscal year 2003 for these projects could limit that authorization to just the $94 million associated with those four seismic jobs.

The physical infrastructure of the VA health care system is one of the largest in the Federal Government. While some VA facilities are relatively new, the average age of VA buildings is 50 years.

During the past few years, there has been a reluctance to commit to capital investment out of a concern that the VA was unsure of facilities that would clearly be needed in the future. As we complete our CARES initiatives that identify options to improve our health care system and provide better access, infrastructure modifications will create a large number of projects for future funding and authorization.

Section 4 of the bill is entitled Increasing the Threshold for Major Medical Facility Construction Projects.

Subsection (a) increases the dollar threshold that defines a major construction project from its current dollar amount of $4 million to more than $6 million.

Subsection (b) of Section 4 seeks to identify those projects to which the increased threshold applies.

VA is currently reviewing Section 4 of the bill and will provide the committee with our views on this provision at a later time.

Section 5 is entitled the Criteria for Minor Constructions Projects.

The language of this section directs the Secretary to select minor construction projects to improve, replace, renovate, or update facilities to achieve improvements in one or more of the five specific areas.

While this language may have been included to provide guidance to the VA in prioritizing the Department's minor construction projects, it eliminates the discretion that the Secretary now has in identifying those minor construction projects that will best meet the overall needs of the Department.

We believe VA's comprehensive process for selecting minor construction projects will best fulfill VA's mission and make Section 5 of the bill unnecessary. Accordingly, we recommend that it be removed from the bill.

This concludes my views on the bill, and I certainly will be glad to discuss this with the members of the committee. Thank you very much.

[The prepared statement of Mr. Catlett appears on p. 34.]

Mr. BOOZMAN. Col. Gilbreath.

STATEMENT OF COL. DAVID D. GILBREATH

Col. GILBREATH. Mr. Chairman, distinguished members of the committee, it is an honor and a privilege to be here today to talk about how the 3rd Medical Group is working with Alaska VA Health Care System to provide comprehensive, quality health care to the veterans of Alaska.

My comments today will include a brief history of our Joint Venture, describe how it works, and finally, discussion of further opportunities for integration with the VA if they build a clinic adjacent to the 3rd Medical Group hospital.

Alaska's immense size, intimidating terrain, distance from the Continental U.S., and high cost of living present a variety of challenges to delivering health care to the more than 100,000 DOD and VA beneficiaries who live in Alaska.

Alaska is a huge state, as we all know, with a land mass one-fifth the size of the lower 48. Road systems in Alaska are sparse. There's only one two-lane road that connects the State's two largest cities, Anchorage and Fairbanks. This, coupled with the severe weather conditions, makes land travel difficult at best.

Alaska is sparsely populated. The State averages less than one person per square mile, compared to 70 people per square mile in the lower 48.

Nearly 25 percent of Alaskans live in towns or villages that can only be reached by plane or boat. Twenty-five percent of Alaskans live in communities with fewer than 1,000 people. The vast majority of the State's physicians reside in the Anchorage bowl area, which has nearly half of the State's population of approximately 650,000.

Many Alaskan communities are medically underserved. For example, hundreds of small villages scattered around the State rely on health aides with an eight grade education as their sole source of primary care. Incredibly, outside Anchorage, there isn't a single practicing cardiologist anywhere in the State.

All these factors contribute to the high cost of health care in Alaska and add to the complexities of providing health care to VA and DOD beneficiaries in this environment.

The VA has never had an inpatient medical facility in Alaska. They have always bought their inpatient services from the private sector.

In 1986, an economic analysis by the Army Corps of Engineers concluded that a cost-effective health care delivery alternative for veterans in the Anchorage area was a DOD/VA joint venture with the Air Force at Elmendorf Air Force Base.

The VA contributed over $11 million toward construction of a $164 million, 110-bed, almost a half-million square foot medical facility at Elmendorf Air Force Base. Construction began in 1993 and the birth of the Elmendorf DOD/VA Joint Venture occurred in May of 1999, nearly 3 years ago, when the 3rd Medical Group cut the ribbon on its new medical facility.

Ours is one of eight DOD/VA joint ventures and it's been the focus of national attention, really, since its inception. It was called a "model for the rest of the country" by VA Secretary Principi during a visit to Alaska last year.

The Joint Venture's principles of operations call for an integrated, jointly staffed medical facility to meet the health care needs of DOD and VA beneficiaries. The VA staffs the intensive care unit and the Air Force staffs the Medical-Surgical Unit.

Since February 1, 2000, the VA also has provided staffing to augment our ER. On that date, the Joint Venture became the ER of choice for Anchorage veterans.

This has been a huge success, because historical data showed that over 25 percent of ER visits of veterans in Anchorage hospitals resulted in an admission. Veterans requiring admission from the ER now are admitted to the Joint Venture hospital, rather than costly hospitals in the private sector.

The Air Force runs the hospital on a day-to-day basis with input from the VA on various committees. The VA reimburses the Air Force for services provided on a per diem basis for inpatient care, and on a fee-schedule basis for outpatient visits and ancillary services, like lab and X-ray, and things like that.

Currently, the VA employs approximately 50 staff members at the Joint Venture. This compares to about 800 staff and another 150 contractors provided by the Air Force.

A major goal of the Joint Venture is to increase access to medical care for veterans, while containing costs. During fiscal year 2001, over 700 veterans were admitted to the Joint Venture hospital. That's a 24 percent increase from the previous year. During that same period, emergency room visits increased 19 percent to almost 2,000 patients.

Because of differing accounting systems between DOD and the VA, it's difficult to really compute what that cost avoidance would be.

The Elmendorf Joint Venture strives to make a seamless continuum of inpatient care, as well as selected outpatient care available to Alaska's veterans, while enhancing the range of services available to DOD beneficiaries.

The Joint Venture is designed to improve the health care delivery system for all eligible federal beneficiaries. It offers VA beneficiaries a local, federal inpatient facility, while DOD beneficiaries enjoy expanded access to specialty care, including ICU, cardiology, and others provided by the VA, and we wouldn't have that if it were not for the Joint Venture, the DOD side.

Special emphasis has been put into place to ensure one standard of care for all patients that receive care at the Joint Venture. Staff from both agencies work very hard to overcome cultural and mission differences to ensure that we meet the common goal of, "Take care of the men and women who have served and continue to serve this great nation."

During our March 2002, just a few weeks ago, Joint Commission on Accreditation of Health Care Organizations visit—that's an accrediting body that really accredits virtually every hospital in the country, including DOD—surveyors praised the Joint Venture for its cost-effectiveness and adherence to one standard of care.

The VA's proposed clinic adjacent to the 3rd Medical Group offers significant opportunities for further integration of services that really currently are not feasible because of proximity. To date, we've held nine separate planning meetings between the Air Force and VA to look at some opportunities. The intent is to share services, integrate services, and reduce the scope of that project in this bill.

Preliminary results are very encouraging. Many areas have been identified as having excess capacity for sharing with the VA. So far, our warehouse, radiology, medical lab, central sterile supply, medical library, and also ambulatory surgery, which was not in my previous written statement, have been identified as potential for integration.

Sharing in these areas should significantly reduce the need for these services in the new VA clinic, thereby producing significant savings in the final scope of that project.

Also, building a VA outpatient clinic adjacent to the 3rd Medical Group offers some significant cost economies of scale through joint housekeeping contracts, shared maintenance contracts, and so on.

Also, an adjacent clinic would present opportunities to share things like biomedical equipment repair with the VA.

It should be pointed out that a huge factor that inhibits more complete integration is incompatible information management systems between the two agencies.

It has been frequently identified that the lack of compatibility between the VA clinical information system and DOD's Composite Health Care System provides a huge roadblock in efficiently integrating operations. In many cases, such duplication often causes redundant data entry and wasted man-hours.

For example, because of incompatible information systems, near-term integration of pharmacy services appears impractical until further technology solutions are developed. However, the DOD and VA are actively working to improve information sharing between medical data systems, and I would cite one example of that being the government computerized patient record.

I am confident that construction of new VA clinic within the immediate proximity of the 3rd Medical Group will further improve our abilities to share resources and services.

Land is available—that's federal land—for construction and it's adjacent to our facility, and it's excess to the needs of the base.

While concerns over security and access have increased since September 11, 2001, recent meetings with Air Force Security Forces and other security personnel have helped devise a plan where access to health care for veterans is ensured while maintaining the security posture essential to protecting the critical security assets based on Elmendorf Air Force Base.

I believe, in conclusion, that a new VA clinic built adjacent to the 3rd Medical Group will dramatically improve access—timely, cost-effective access—for veterans in Alaska. The men and women of the 3rd Medical Group are eager and poised to make that happen. This will definitely be a win for the VA, a win for DOD, and a huge win for the American taxpayer.

Mr. Chairman, distinguished members of the committee, thank you for this opportunity to report on the challenges and successes of our Joint Venture, and thank you for the continued advocacy and support for our Nation's veterans.

I would be happy to answer any questions.

[The prepared statement of Col. Gilbreath appears on p. 38.]

Mr. BOOZMAN. Thank you. Dr. Filner.

OPENING STATEMENT OF HON. BOB FILNER

Mr. FILNER. Thank you, Mr. Chairman. I would just ask unanimous consent to have my opening statement made part of the record, and I just also want to welcome my good friend, Mr. Rossio, from San Diego. He, of course, is the CEO of the VA's San Diego Health Care System, and he is universally recognized throughout our community as a real advocate for veterans, and one who works hard.

We've put him in the position of having to keep doing more with less, he does a very good job at it, and he's recognized nationally for that, so welcome, Mr. Rossio, or Gary, if I may, and you're welcome to add any remarks that you would like.

You know, San Diego is authorized in the bill under consideration. Also, I don't know if it was made clear, although the President only put in his budget room for four projects, we have, 10 in the bill.

So we hope to make sure all these projects are funded.

Welcome to Washington.

[The prepared statement of Congressman Filner appears on p. 27.]

Mr. ROSSIO. Can I make a comment now?

Mr. BOOZMAN. Sure.

Mr. ROSSIO. Okay. I'll be glad to do that. It's an honor to see this august body, and Mr. Filner, once again. I see him fairly often, as you can tell.

Just a little background about the San Diego VA Hospital itself. It was designed in 1967 and constructed between 1969 and 1971, and we admitted our first patient March 15, 1972, so we just had our 30-year anniversary just last month, so we've been in business all this time, and it has about 850,000 square feet.

The project for the seismic basin itself was based on a code deficiency, because we are now in Earthquake Zone Number 4, and the hospital is built on the Rose Canyon Fault.

The project was designed to retrofit the current structure to bring it up to life safety standards, so that it can not only withstand an earthquake, but be operational after an earthquake, so I think that's a significant difference from some of your other codes over time, because I think if the building is standing, we intend to keep occupying it.

So the 47,000 patients that we now treat through that facility during the course of a year is expanding at a rate of about 15 percent per year, so over the next life of that building, in the next 15 or 20 years, we'll be able to pick up quite a bit of the 360,000 veterans who live in our county.

The project itself is 100 percent about seismic upgrading. I think you know the value of the project, it's in the bill, and the opportunity that this presents for us would, I think, guarantee the safety of our staff, which is about 2,000 people, about 1,000 volunteers, and of course on any given day, we'll have three or four thousand people in that building that are patients coming through that place.

I would be glad to—I could tell you a couple things. The census in the hospital is about 170 patients per day, which includes a 40-bed nursing home care unit, a 30-bed spinal cord injury unit. We are a Southwest Referral Site for bypass surgery, for spinal cord injury.

We also have a teaching mission with the University of California San Diego of 147 house officers there on an annual basis.

We do have a $50 million research program between the VA and the National Institutes of Health, and we do back up the Department of Defense. That's our fourth mission.

We have a very close working relationship with the Navy Balboa, and have done several joint ventures over time, and plan to do some more.

But I think our need is to maintain the structural strength of the building and be able to provide patients and our staff safety over time in the event of a major earthquake, which is—you know, the big joke out there is, buy ocean front property in Nevada.

Well, the boomer is coming one of these days at some point in time. We hope to not be there when it's there, but at the same time, we hope this will stand up to that earthquake if it ever hits.

I'll take some questions now if you'd like me to.

Mr. BOOZMAN. Thank you, Mr. Rossio. Mr. Neary, do you have any comments?

Mr. NEARY. No, sir.

Mr. BOOZMAN. Okay. Mr. Spector.

Mr. SPECTOR. Thank you, Mr. Chairman. Thank you for having us here today. I have no comments for the written record.

I would like to thank Col. Gilbreath for attending here, and I concur in his comments and our good working relationship.

Mr. BOOZMAN. Thank you very much. We certainly appreciate your testimony.

Mr. Catlett, you mentioned earlier that many of our structures are 50 years old, and, you know, becoming quite, quite aged.

You also said that part of that reason was because we hadn't really decided, you know, in the years, as to whether or not what was going to be utilized, didn't really have a plan.

Mr. CATLETT. Right.

Mr. BOOZMAN. Are we starting to address that now? Do we have a plan in the future to know which areas that we want to maintain and which areas aren't going to be needed? Are we working in that area?

Mr. CATLETT. Well, Mr. Chairman, through the program we've identified as CARES. As you may know, we completed and the Secretary approved the recommendations for what we call the pilot Phase 1, which is the pilot in the Chicago-Wisconsin area.

With the Secretary's insistence towards speeding up the process for the rest of the Nation, we are actively preparing for that.

So I guess the direct answer to your question is no, we don't have that completed. From your view and from many of ours, we have not had the funding that we've needed to maintain the infrastructure.

But from oversight in both ends of the street, both in the Executive Branch and in the Congress, the challenge that has been placed to us is to define our future, which most people recognize is a significantly smaller physical infrastructure, because of the changes in medicine, in particular, in the way medicine is practiced. We have that challenge to complete.

We're hoping that very soon we will be announcing the implementation of the next phase of CARES, and certainly we're interested in doing this, in speeding it up.

We would complete the rest of the country in the next step, in developing a proposal, obviously, that will require a lot of vetting with veterans' groups and with the Congress, and we'll hopefully be providing specific details on that soon.

I'll give you some more general details, if you're interested.

Mr. BOOZMAN. Thank you. Are you familiar with our Chairman's bill, H.R. 2667, to enhance VA/DOD sharing, with some of the provisions in that bill such as DOD's use of VA hiring for authorities for clinicians in Title 38? Would the mandate to coordinate care for both veterans and DOD beneficiaries on one site be helpful to the new Joint Venture in Anchorage?

I guess that would be Mr. Spector, perhaps Mr. Gilbreath.

Mr. SPECTOR. I'm not familiar with the contents of the bill, sir, but certainly the partnership that we have in Anchorage with Elmendorf Air Force Base would go a long ways towards those ideas of more sharing and working together with veterans and DOD beneficiaries to assure that there's an adequate site for their care.

We have been able to make a lot of arrangements among ourselves, joint policy letters we call them, operating agreements, that assures that access to care, whether you're a DOD beneficiary or a VA beneficiary is achieved at our site, access to beds, also.

So I think that, without knowing the contents of the bill particularly, I think that our Joint Venture in Alaska has been demonstrated as a model of a good working relationship and we hope to continue that in the future.

Mr. BOOZMAN. Mr. Filner.

Mr. FILNER. Thank you, Mr. Chairman.

Mr. Catlett, I was just wondering if you might explain to us the rationale behind the list that you have created for priority projects.

For example, as Mr. Rossio stated, the San Diego medical complex sits basically on an earthquake fault, and yet it's behind projects which are not—they're projects that have nothing to do with earthquakes or don't seem to face the same kind of risk that San Diego does.

You have recommended, or the President recommended several areas in California for construction. I'm not sure why they are any more risky than San Diego.

I'm not saying they ought not to be built. They ought to. But what's going into the ranking system here, where such an obvious candidate is ranked well below some others that are not so obvious?

Mr. CATLETT. Mr. Filner, in addition to the list I believe you're referring to, a list of 20 projects submitted, as important as that list is, there was a list about 2 years ago, at the request of FEMA, on exceptionally high-risk buildings due to seismic conditions. The projects that we requested of OMB, and submitted, included San Diego, and we followed that list in terms of the projects that we were recommending.

San Diego, as you note, is very near the top of that list. It was the fourth of the major projects that we had identified in our request.

Frankly, it was a numbers game. The 1, 2, 3, and 5 were selected to fit within the funds that we had available to us. San Diego was the more expensive of those five projects, and in the negotiations to get to a budget to be submitted for 2003 for our construction account, we had to fit within the number, of $94 million, and so we tried to get as many projects as we could.

Mr. FILNER. I realize we have a scarcity of resources. Are these the top 20 that you submitted to the President?

Mr. CATLETT. Well, again, the list largely followed that.

What it gets back to is the CARES question as noted. We've been unsuccessful, basically, in getting a lot of projects.

The last 4 years before this budget was submitted, for the projects for our health care system in major construction, the average amount requested was $43 million.

The last 2 years, we had one project each. One of them was not approved by the Congress, and we were lucky to get last year's project.

So as everyone has been waiting for CARES, we've been trying to make the case that there are patient safety risks that we need to address, and seismic, we think, has been the most significant.

We have submitted a much longer list to OMB, but when you get to the negotiations on this—and again, I'm not laying this on OMB. I understand their perspective. I understand the perspective that exists here.

But we have emphasized for several years that they are patient safety factors that need to be considered while we're waiting to complete the CARES process, particularly seismic.

Frankly, to get four in, when the past 2 years had one each, was a significant improvement, although well below where we should be funding the system for renovation.

Mr. FILNER. I appreciate that, and I'm grateful. It's going to be a catch-up game for several years, even if we fund the projects in this bill adequately. There is a deep safety issue here. Mr. Rossio, for example, has several thousand people in a building that's right on an earthquake fault.

I appreciate what you said. I hope our committee looks favorably at this bill, and when we get to the budget, adequately appropriates what we need.

I thank you, sir.

Mr. BOOZMAN. Mr. Brown.

OPENING STATEMENT OF HON. HENRY E. BROWN

Mr. BROWN. Mr. Chairman, thank you for bringing this to our attention.

I'm from Charleston, SC in the First Congressional District. We have some 70,000 veterans, and we certainly are concerned about it.

I know last Monday, Mr. Buyer and myself took a tour of the Navy Hospital and the Veterans Hospital and also the medical university with the thought of maybe trying to better care for the health needs of our veterans and also our military personnel, by combining those services.

I'm anxious to see that, in this bill, they have one in Alaska that's going to basically address a joint use. This is what we have for the idea for South Carolina. We certainly would hope that this committee would give us some consideration, too.

I know it looks like it's pretty slanted to two or three states, and I'm sure that there's limited resources, but we would like to be considered in the not-too-distant future to become a pilot project sort of like the one in Alaska.

So Mr. Chairman, with that in mind, I would like to just submit my opening statement with these concerns attached.

Mr. BOOZMAN. Without objection.

[The prepared statement of Congressman Brown appears on p. 29.]

Mr. CATLETT. Mr. Chairman, if I could——

Mr. BOOZMAN. Sure.——

Mr. CATLETT (continuing). Just a comment for Mr. Brown.

Obviously, the President identified a task force to improve VA/DOD planning, particularly for health care, I would add as well that, while that's a 2-year project, our deputy secretary, Dr. McKay, has initiated an executive council with Dr. Chu of DOD, and clearly, coordination of joint medical ventures is high on that list.

So that is something that the department has been working with DOD actively.

Look, I can't speak to any specific project, but clearly the overall approach and the recognition of opportunities for joint ventures is something that is being pursued vigorously.

Mr. BOOZMAN. Ms. Berkley.

OPENING STATEMENT OF HON. SHELLEY BERKLEY

Ms. BERKLEY. I'm obviously going to support this legislation. I think it's very important.

But I also feel I would be remiss if I didn't bring up yet again the problems I'm having in southern Nevada. In addition to not having our own hospital, and I know Mr. Brown spoke of having 70,000 veterans, I've got 270,000 veterans, no hospital.

The VA clinic, as you know, is going to be closed down because we have such significant structural damage that it is no longer safe to go into the building. We have no idea if it is repairable, and we're looking for a temporary site at this point, but I'm going to need some relief, and it's more than just slight improvements on the structures. We need facilities in southern Nevada, and the money has got to follow the veterans.

So, having said that, I will support this legislation. I know that there are VA facilities across the United States that are struggling to keep up with the needs that they already have, and that there are serious structural problems with many of the existing facilities, but not only do I have an existing facility now that is unusable, I have no facility—no hospital facility, no long-term care facility—and I would hope that we would be able to make a determination of which facilities are no longer functional, which facilities can be closed, without compromising the health care of veterans on the East Coast, but let that money come to the West Coast and to the western states, where we have an incredible influx of veterans with no facilities to care for them.

So thank you very much for being here. I know you've got a tough job.

I will help you with yours. I would appreciate it if you would help me with mine.

[The prepared statement of Congresswoman Berkley appears on p. 31.]

Mr. CATLETT. Yes, ma'am. Thank you.

Mr. BOOZMAN. Thank you. Mr. Miller?

Mr. MILLER. Thank you, Mr. Chairman. I, too, have a statement I'd like to add into the record, and I have just a question and a comment.

[The prepared statement of Congressman Miller appears on p. 32.]

Mr. MILLER. Mr. Catlett, did VISN 16 convey any need for a medical center or an additional clinic in Northwest Florida to your knowledge?

Mr. CATLETT. Sixteen?

Mr. MILLER. Sixteen, yeah.

Mr. CATLETT. Not that I'm aware of, but I will check that and make that available for the record——

Mr. MILLER. Thank you.

Mr. CATLETT. For the 2003 process, I'm not familiar that they did.

Mr. MILLER. Also, I, too, as my colleagues Mr. Brown and Ms. Berkley, am interested in the joint use type facility, and I'd like to have my staff be able to contact you, Mr. Spector, or Col. Gilbreath, to talk about the issue.

I have 109,000 veterans in my First Congressional District, almost half of the total number in 16, and I, too, do not have a hospital for them to go to, as well, but we have a couple of DOD facilities, and it would be a great potential for a joint use facility there, as well.

Thank you for coming today. I appreciate it.

Mr. BOOZMAN. Thank you.

Col. Gilbreath, in the past, we've had a little bit of a problem, commanding officer rotation has been reported as a serious problem for continued VA/DOD health sharing.

If you and the VA director move to new assignments before the project comes to fruition, before, you know, we really get on the stick and get this thing going, will this initiative need to be restarted, or it might die because its originators are not on the scene to keep it alive?

That has been a little bit of a problem in the past. Do you foresee a problem in the future with that?

Col. GILBREATH. Mr. Chairman, as you know, most commanders move about every 2 years. I think there's more stability in the VA system; but typically, commanders move every 2 years, and there are some exceptions to that.

Concerning the particular project, the Joint Venture in Anchorage, I think there's commitment throughout the organization and I don't think it's just from the commander down. In fact, I talked about the Joint Venture with my replacement, who will be coming in later this summer, and after some discussion, he's convinced it's the right thing to do.

I think when you look at this from the federal taxpayer viewpoint, and it makes a lot of sense. It's not easy to convince your staff that it's the right thing to do.

There are some exceptions to that, and that would be the low-ranking person that all they see is once in a while they come in and work a little harder, because there's more patients in the bed, or they work an extra shift when there's a lack of beds or lack of staff to take care of the patients that come in.

But, no. I think—I don't think we're anywhere close to having to start this over with a change in leadership at the 3rd Medical Group.

Mr. BOOZMAN. Very good.

Mr. SPECTOR. Could I comment, Mr. Boozman?

Mr. BOOZMAN. Yes, sir.

Mr. SPECTOR. In addition to what Col. Gilbreath has said, I think there is a potential, with personalities commanding either the VA or the DOD facility, it's personality-driven at times, but we have also set into place in our Joint Venture an infrastructure of committees which have both VA and Air Force personnel on them, so we are intertwined together on quality of care issues, safety issues, space issues, environmental care issues.

In addition, we have what we call our Joint Venture Business Operations Committee, which has equal membership between the Air Force and the VA, which addresses the day-to-day operational issues and these integration issues that we talked about that Col. Gilbreath presented to you.

So we have a structure in place below the command level that does the business of the Joint Venture that will keep it going when the commanders do change, if they do change.

Mr. BOOZMAN. Thank you. Dr. Filner.

[No response.]

Mr. BOOZMAN. Ms. Berkley?

[No response.]

Mr. BOOZMAN. I want to thank you all so much for coming. I know you've come a long way, many of you, and we really do appreciate your testimony and insight.

We'll have some follow-up written questions. So thank you very much.

Let's go to Panel 2 now, Mr. Antonio Laracuente, Dr. Donald Wilson, thank you all for being with us today.

Mr. Laracuente is chairman of the National Association of Veterans' Research and Education Foundations of Atlanta, Georgia, who is offering testimony on behalf of the Executive Committee, Friends of VA Medical Care and Health Research; and Dr. Donald E. Wilson, vice president for medical affairs and dean of the University of Maryland School of Medicine, who is offering testimony on behalf of the Association of American Medical Colleges.

Let's proceed. Yes, sir.

STATEMENTS OF ANTONIO LARACUENTE, CHAIRMAN, NATIONAL ASSOCIATION OF VETERANS' RESEARCH AND EDUCATION FOUNDATIONS (NAVREF) ON BEHALF OF THE FRIENDS OF VA MEDICAL CARE AND HEALTH RESEARCH (FOVA) AND DONALD E. WILSON, M.D., VICE PRESIDENT FOR MEDICAL AFFAIRS AND DEAN, UNIVERSITY OF MARYLAND SCHOOL OF MEDICINE, ON BEHALF OF THE ASSOCIATION OF AMERICAN MEDICAL COLLEGES (AAMC)

STATEMENT OF ANTONIO LARACUENTE

Mr. LARACUENTE. Thank you, Mr. Chairman and members of the subcommittee, for the opportunity to present testimony.

I am Antonio Laracuente, executive director of the Atlanta Research and Education Foundation, and I am here today as chairman of the National Association of Veterans' Research and Education Foundations on behalf of the Friends of VA Medical Care and Health Research.

We applaud this subcommittee for its leadership, not just in supporting the research program, but in securing House passage of H.R. 811, the Veterans' Hospital Emergency Repair Act, and for incorporating in that bill an allocation to upgrade and renovate VA's research facilities.

The bill came close to accomplishing what I am here to ask for today, a dedicated funding stream for renovation and repair of VA's existing research facilities.

The VA research program is of consistently high quality and remarkably productive. Despite shortcomings in the research facilities, every week the press reports medical breakthroughs by VA researchers that make a positive impact on the health of every American.

However, I believe VA is reaching the point where a significant investment in the research infrastructure is essential. The current practice of allocating all minor constructing funding to one appropriation no longer serves VA facilities well.

Congress has mandated that VA provide care and conduct research, yet construction funding for both is provided in one appropriation they distributed largely on the basis of clinical relevance at both the central office and VISN levels. Research cannot, and we feel should not, compete with medical center needs for renovation and patient care areas.

However, in recent years, the minor construction appropriation has been chronically inadequate to meet even high priority clinical needs, so little, if anything, is left over for research.

Network and medical center directors make an effort to search out funding for research facilities, cutting a little here and there, and in some cases relying on the affiliated universities and research foundations to contribute to the most basic necessary renovations.

However, funding for long overdue renovations is the exception, not the rule. The medical care appropriation is severely strained. The affiliates have their own funding priorities and few of the research corporations have the resources to fill the gaps.

When money can be scraped together, all too often the amount is inadequate to meet facility-wide needs, such as a new venting and air conditioning system for the animal facility, or project-specific needs such as upgrading a lab to biosafety level three, which is essential for the Hepatitis C and HIV research projects so relevant to our veteran patients.

The lack of a systematic approach to funding these needs is unacceptable for a world-class research program.

VA research laboratories are falling into disrepair, and are increasingly unable to accommodate modern science. Many appear to be on the brink of jeopardizing patient, staff, and animal safety.

When an animal facility is too small, investigators bring the animals into their regular laboratories, exposing themselves and staff to occupational illnesses. OSHA inspectors have expressed concerns, and in one case said that if it were up to OSHA, the building would be shut down.

During an annual inspection, a fire marshal recommended that research laboratories no longer be housed in one building, because the building lacks fire sensors and sprinkler systems.

Backup generators are needed to ensure safe temperatures in animal facilities on hot days.

During a hazardous materials drill last December, a local fire department spread banana oil to mimic a toxic spill. Within 15 minutes, oil applied on the fourth floor of the research building was identified on the second and fourth floors of the adjoining patient care facility.

VA research personnel are extremely creative problem solvers, but they are using bandaid solutions. I believe VA is reaching a crisis point at many facilities across the country.

Thanks, in large part, to this subcommittee, the VA research appropriation has grown, and we hope it will continue to do so in 2003, and beyond.

Concurrently, VA investigators are remarkably successful in competing for NIH and other federal awards as well as private sector grants. However, expansion of VA research facilities has not kept pace with the increase in the number of projects conducted by VA investigators. This has created an urgent need for new research space.

In some cases, a new building is warranted. In others, conversion of former wards into research laboratories is a better solution, but funding is unavailable.

I suspect that every research office across the Nation maintains a list of urgently needed repairs, improvements, and expansion needs. Unfortunately, at most facilities, the lists get longer each year.

To address this tremendous backlog and establish reliable resources in the future, Friends of VA urges this subcommittee to establish a funding stream specifically for research facility improvements. This would recognize that both research and medical care have essential, but often distinct and differing, construction needs.

We recommend central management of the funds by the Office of Research and Development so the most pressing needs can be prioritized among large and small upgrades, as well as facility-wide and with project-specific needs.

The VA has a list of 15 priority sites and in need of significant renovation with price tags ranging from $1 million to nearly $4 million. Some involve replacing inadequate buildings while others provide for renovation of existing space.

These add up to $42 million, close to the Friends of VA recommendation of $45 million. FOVA would like to see the additional $3 million reserved for smaller, project-specific needs.

We urge this subcommittee to authorize a centrally administered, dedicated funding steam specifically for improvements in VA's research facilities.

We sincerely appreciate that research is incorporated in H.R. 4514, the Veterans' Major Medical Facilities Construction Act of 2002, but we are concerned that research needs may be relegated to the bottom of the priority list, and will remain unfunded.

In our view, research facilities should be on a separate priority list with explicitly designated funding.

Thank you for your consideration.

[The prepared statement of Mr. Laracuente appears on p. 42.]

Mr. FILNER. Mr. Chairman, if I may intervene, I thank Mr. Catlett for staying, and I'll ask the question at the end of Dr. Wilson's testimony, but in the written testimony that Mr. Laracuente submitted to us, he talked about the VA, the lack of add-on from NIH for research, the real overhead costs, and I'm just wondering why we haven't been able to get that from NIH, if you can answer that later.

Let Dr. Wilson, if that's under your purview, I'd like you to go into that issue, because I read Mr. Laracuente's testimony and it just seems obvious that that should occur, but I'll go into it later.

Thank you, Mr. Chairman.

Mr. BOOZMAN. Dr. Wilson.

STATEMENT OF DONALD E. WILSON

Dr. WILSON. Mr. Chairman, members of the committee, thank you for the invitation to be here today.

I'm immediate past chair of the Council of Deans of our Nation's medical schools, and I'm also a veteran. Today I'm representing the Association of American Medical Colleges, the AAMC.

The AAMC represents the Nation's 125 accredited allopathic medical schools, over 400 major teaching hospitals and health systems, including 72 Veterans' Affairs Medical Centers, 98 academic and scientific societies representing over 100,000 faculty, the Nation's 66,000 medical students, and 97,000 residents.

As I'm sure you know, 107 of those 125 medical schools maintain formal affiliation agreements with VA medical centers and these agreements are mutually beneficial to both the academic partner and the VA in each of the VA's major missions of patient care, research, and education.

The VA's research programs enhance the value of an affiliation, with schools of medicine, improving collaboration, and providing an important tool for recruiting high-quality faculty and staff, not only to the medical school but to the VA.

Currently, VA research facility renovations are funded through the minor construction account, where they have to compete with clinical needs. There are countless examples of dilapidated and inadequate VA research facilities, some of which led universities to delay ongoing research, or even stop responding to program announcements.

Top researchers at some universities and VA medical centers are citing poor-quality VA research facilities as a major reason for leaving the site and going elsewhere.

There are also some good examples of partnerships between the VA and academic affiliates, such as at Penn State and Texas A&M, which are further detailed in my written statement.

With my own VA affiliation in Baltimore, we're in drastic need of about 20,000 net square feet of research space, just to meet our current needs. Even though the existing building was only completed in 1993, it was based on designs that took into account research funding from the 1970s. Funding had increased more than eight-fold by the time construction was completed.

This year, researchers at the VA Maryland Health Center System have been awarded about $12.5 million in VA research funding and an additional $20.5 million in non-VA funding for a total research enterprise of $33 million.

Because of a lack of space, at least 18 of these researchers are being housed in medical school laboratories at the medical school's expense.

These kind of relationships are only possible because of the close working relationship that we have between myself and the Baltimore VA Medical Center.

The most viable option to solve our space problem is to purchase additional space that could be used jointly by the VA and the University of Maryland School of Medicine.

In a VA Central Office survey, the Baltimore VA Medical Center ranked second nationally in research construction need with a price tag of about $3.5 million just to ameliorate the current space crunch. However, minor construction and renovation projects like this one must compete with some of the clinical needs of the VA health system.

Now, I would not suggest that the research facility needs should outweigh the needs of the clinical program, but I would suggest that a better process is needed so that research facility needs are not consistently left at the bottom of the list.

The importance of the VA affiliation to the research program is not limited to facility issues. The geriatrics division at the University of Maryland School of Medicine is totally housed at our VA, and our new state-of-the-art cardiovascular exercise research facility is housed at the VA, even though the medical school funded 87 percent of the cost.

The VA will soon have a human performance laboratory to look at such things as gait analysis to help diagnose and treat patients suffering with movement disorders and stroke.

Additionally, a significant portion of the Parkinson's disease and multiple sclerosis research that goes on at the School of Medicine is located at the VA.

Again, I cannot stress enough that these types of relationships are mutually beneficial to both the VA and the School of Medicine, and the ultimate benefits go to the patients, but the full potential of our relationship cannot be realized, because the VA research facilities are inadequate.

For the affiliation partnership to flourish, resources need to come from both partners. Currently, the biggest need on the VA side is research space, and I believe that a dedicated funding source for VA research facilities that does not compete with clinical needs is necessary to further our shared goals.

Let me conclude by saying it is well-documented that the affiliation between VA and universities improve patient care as well as the education of the next generation of our Nation's health care professionals. The value of research to the affiliations, the subject of today's hearing, is not as well known.

My affiliation in Baltimore is not unique. Many, if not most, of the Nation's VA researchers hold joint faculty appointments at an affiliated medical school.

In order for these affiliations to be as effective as possible, the facilities in which the research is conducted need to be state-of-the-art.

We're all aware that patient care needs create a strain on the VA medical care budget. However, VA research facilities should not be forced to compete against these clinical needs, nor should they be ignored.

We support a separate funding stream for the renovation of VA research facilities that does not compete with directly with clinical needs.

Thank you for your attention, and I'll be willing to answer any questions that you might have.

[The prepared statement of Mr. Wilson appears on p. 47.]

Mr. BOOZMAN. Thank you. I guess I just have, really, just kind of a question/comment, and I think I know the answer, after hearing your testimony.

But certainly, the VA research is and has been a wonderful thing. Is it going to continue to be so, you know, if we don't solve our infrastructure problems, as you've outlined?

Dr. WILSON. I've been dean at Maryland for 10½ years and I'm now finding it increasingly difficult to get high-quality investigators to come to our VA.

Mr. BOOZMAN. Thank you. Dr. Filner.

Mr. FILNER. Thank you. As I said, I don't think you went into it in your oral testimony, but it was in your written testimony. I thank you both for your comments.

Is it Laracuente? Am I pronouncing it right?

Mr. LARACUENTE. Yes, sir.

Mr. FILNER. Can you just explain what you call the 15 percent VA add-on situation with NIH——

Mr. LARACUENTE. Yes, sir.

Mr. FILNER (continuing). And the problem there?

Mr. LARACUENTE. Currently, any work that is performed at the VA Medical Center that is administered by the university receives what is deemed an off-campus rate, which is capped at 26 percent of indirect costs of the negotiated rate with NIH, the university negotiated rate with NIH.

The VA houses the program, basically uses its facilities to run these programs, and receives no support for these programs from the university or from the NIH.

We have, for the past 6 or 7 years, been working with the VA to try to negotiate with the NIH what is called the 15 percent add-on.

It is our understanding that only the Department of Health and Human Services policy change is needed for this, and basically it seems that the VA and the NIH cannot come together to reach an agreement on this simple—well, what we feel is a very simple and fair issue.

Mr. FILNER. But other institutions get this add-on?

Mr. LARACUENTE. It's our understanding that the VA does not get this add-on, so——

Mr. FILNER. But do others? If it was granted to a university investigator——

Mr. LARACUENTE. If the award is granted to the university, and the work is performed at the university, then they get the add-on facilities cost. The VA does not.

Mr. FILNER. Mr. Catlett, again, I thank you for staying for the extra panel.

If you might, in Mr. Laracuente's testimony, he says that this has been an ongoing discussion for 6 or 7 years, and I'm wondering what the problem is. Does it need a legislative fix?

Is it just that, HHS doesn't want to give up the money? What is going on there?

Mr. CATLETT. Mr. Filner, I can't give you the complete answer. I'll fill in what I know, but we will provide for the record. The best source, I think, would be Dr. Feussner who heads a research program within the VA health administration.

In fact, the reason I can speak now and give you a few points is I spoke with him for more than a half hour, no more than 2 weeks ago, on this issue, in sort of getting up to speed.

Apparently, before 1989, we did receive it, but we don't any longer, and apparently that had something to do with the VA initiative, due to problems with the administration of those funds.

I know that the VA, if not VHA, has written recently, and again requested that we get this indirect cost markup, as I call it. I believe we've been rejected in the first response, but I understand we intend to pursue it.

To complicate it, one other fact that I know, believe I know; the VA research corporations, in their research proposals, they get that markup.

Again, what we're talking about is mostly the same researchers, whether they're affiliated with the university, the VA, or with research corporations, and in two out of the three cases, the indirect markup happens, but it doesn't happen when it's a VA initiated research.

So we are pursuing this as a department, and we will provide for you, as quick as you'd like, but certainly for the record, a complete explanation of sort of the current status.

(See p. 21.)

Mr. FILNER. I appreciate that, and please keep us informed, because if we have to say something as a committee or a Congress, it seems to me a no-brainer.

Mr. CATLETT. Right.

Mr. FILNER. And that would give, as Mr. Laracuente calculated, almost $30 million to our researchers, and that's not the whole solution——

Mr. CATLETT. Right.

Mr. FILNER (continuing). But it adds to our research budget.

Mr. CATLETT. We agree.

Mr. FILNER. There are several, of these inter-departmental kinds of things, it seems, that we ought to be working on. What we call Medicare subvention is another. The VA could be raised in its quality and actually save our own government money.

Mr. CATLETT. Exactly.

Mr. FILNER. And we're not doing it.

Mr. CATLETT. Hopefully, this one is easier to solve than Medicare subvention.

Mr. FILNER. Okay. If you let us know, so——

Mr. CATLETT. But it is a hill to climb.

Mr. FILNER. If you let us know what is going on, so we can——

Mr. CATLETT. You bet. We sure will.

Mr. FILNER (continuing). Help that if we have to, and Mr. Chairman, maybe we, after we get the information as a committee, might try to at least have the HHS tell us what's going on and respond to us to see if we need any legislative action.

I appreciate your bringing it to our attention. Thank you for staying and helping us out there.

Mr. CATLETT. Certainly.

(Subsequently, the Department of Veterans Affairs provided the following information:)

DEPARTMENT OF VETERANS AFFAIRS
Veterans Health Administration
Washington DC 20420

MAY 13 2002

In Reply Refer To: 10/12

The Honorable Bob Filner
Ranking Democratic Member
Subcommittee on Health
Committee on Veterans' Affairs
U.S. House of Representatives
Washington, DC 20515

Dear Congressman Filner:

At the April 24, 2002, HVAC Subcommittee on Health hearing on H.R. 4514, you requested that VA provide a complete explanation and status of VA negotiations with the National Institutes of Health (NIH) for a 15 percent administrative fee to be posted to VA when NIH funds are used by VA staff to support NIH research in VA space. Enclosed is a fact sheet prepared by the VA Office of Research and Development that describes the rationale for, history, and current status of VA negotiations with NIH on the matter. I have also enclosed a copy of the most recent correspondence from the VA Under Secretary for Health to the Acting Director of NIH. No response was received to this letter.

If you have further questions or need additional information, please have a member of your staff contact Dr. John Feussner, Chief Research and Development Officer, at (202) 565-8440.

Robert H. Roswell, M.D.
Under Secretary for Health

Enclosures

Fact Sheet
Addressing a Request from
The Honorable Bob Filner
In Follow up to the April 24 Hearing on H.R. 4514
Before the Subcommittee on Health
House Committee on Veterans' Affairs

Subject: Recovery of incremental indirect costs of NIH grants

1. VA appropriated R&D funds may not be used for services that should be provided as administrative support by the VA health care facility. Among the services not supported by the R&D appropriation are radiation safety, waste disposal, custodial care, safety training and monitoring, library, maintenance and upgrade of research space, telephones and various support services such as warehouse, mail, WOC processing. These facilities and administrative (F&A) costs are paid from the medical care appropriation. NIH and DHHS often refer to these services/costs as Operations and Management (O&M) which is a component of a university F&A rate.

VA facilities incur incremental F&A costs when the volume of research at the facility increases. In the case of **VA-funded** research, an increase in research activity results in an increase in medical care appropriated dollars in support of the research (VERA). However, VERA dollars are a fixed amount that reflects the size of the appropriated R&D budget. Total VERA dollars do not increase in response to an increase in extramurally funded research. The proposed 15%-20% VA add-on to the NIH off-site rate would cover part of the incremental F&A costs for NIH grants conducted at a VA facility. It would apply only in instances when choice and circumstances dictate that the affiliated university acts as the grant recipient and the majority of the work on the individual grant is conducted in a VA facility. The 15%-20% add-on would be added to the university's negotiated off-site rate and provided to the VA facility as a pass through.

2. Prior to 1989, NIH provided a flat 15% indirect cost recovery rate to VA facilities on NIH grants. Since 1989, NIH policy has not allowed reimbursement of F&A costs in grants to Federal facilities. Further, in situations where the NIH grant is made to a university affiliate (rather than directly to VA) but the research is conducted at the VA facility, NIH does not pay the full, negotiated F&A rate to the affiliated university. Typically, the payment is at a lower "off-site" rate reflecting only the university's administrative costs (the A of F&A). .Affiliates have been reluctant to share these funds with VA facilities. The consequence is that an increase in NIH funded research results in incremental F&A costs for the VA facility for which, presently, there is no extramural source of reimbursement.

3. NIH and, more recently, DHSS staff have indicated some receptivity to the concept of a "VA add-on", recognizing that there are some costs attributable to NIH-funded research that are incremental to baseline institutional costs that support the VA research mission and, therefore, are potentially reimbursable. However, NIH staff told VA it must make a formal request for the add-on before NIH will take action. VA made formal requests in Drs. Kizer's (6/17/99) and Garthwaite's (10/4/00) letters to the Director, NIH, but no action was taken. VA's Chief Research and Development Officer, Dr. John R. Feussner met with the NIH Deputy Director, Dr. Wendy Baldwin on Jan. 19, 2001. Dr. Baldwin agreed that time was

ripe for a decision and that she would recommend to institute directors that VA receive reimbursement for incremental facilities costs. Subsequently, Dr. Baldwin presented this concept to the Directors of the 22 NIH Institutes. It was rejected. At the same meeting the Directors approved paying indirect costs to foreign institutions.

4. At current levels of NIH grants to VA researchers, reimbursement of VA F&A costs by NIH at a rate of 15-20% would produce additional revenues of about $25-30 million annually.

5. A previously cited difficulty for obtaining approval for a VA add-on rate is the NIH requirement that institutions account for indirect cost reimbursement. The VA recently produced an indirect cost analysis that demonstrated its ability to account for indirect costs and supported a national add-on rate of 15-20%. The new ability to account for F&A costs should satisfy the NIH requirement to account for NIH indirect costs.

6. The VA add-on would strengthen the university-NIH-VA partnership. Universities still would receive and retain their off-site rate.

7. The add on may represent a net cost benefit to NIH. Presumably, funds accruing to VA via the add on would allow VA to house more NIH-sponsored research in better facilities, reducing the need for universities to build new research facilities. University construction costs are generally passed on to NIH, whereas VA pays its own costs.

The VA Office of Research and Development believes that:

1. The purpose of the VA appropriation is support of VA's intramural research activities.
2. Support for research provided by the medical care appropriation is being stretched too thin by recent growth in extramurally funded research conducted in VA facilities. NIH-sponsored research now represents about one third of the total VA research enterprise.
3. VA has the ability to accept reimbursement for F&A costs from other Federal agencies.
4. NIH has recognized its obligation to reimburse for F&A costs associated with its grants.
5. VA has significantly improved its ability to account for F&A costs and can clearly demonstrate the incremental increase associated with non-VA-funded research.

The concept of a VA add-on has been discussed for years and it is time for DHHS-NIH to reinstate indirect cost reimbursement to VA.

DEPARTMENT OF VETERANS AFFAIRS
Veterans Health Administration
Washington DC 20420

APR 26 2001

In Reply Refer To: 121

Ruth Kirschstein, M.D.
Acting Director
National Institutes of Health
9000 Rockville Pike
Bethesda, MD 20892

Dear Dr. Kirschstein:

It is my understanding that on March 1, 2001, the National Institutes of Health (NIH) directors dismissed the concept of reimbursing Veterans Affairs (VA) for the incremental costs of conducting NIH-funded research in VA facilities when such grants are administered by affiliated universities. This action occurred despite a positive recommendation from Dr. Wendy Baldwin, Deputy Director for Extramural Research. I am disappointed by NIH's position on this issue and the prospect that resolution may be further delayed.

On several occasions, the Veterans Health Administration (VHA) and its stakeholders have provided comprehensive data demonstrating that reimbursement for incremental indirect costs to VA facilities is allowable, defensible and needed. Public Law 90-31, Sec. 507, states: "Appropriations to the Public Health Service available for research, training, or demonstration project grants pursuant to this Act shall also be available, on the same terms and conditions as apply to non-Federal institutions, for grants for the same purpose to hospitals ... of the Veterans Administration." Moreover, the Economy Act and OMB Circular No. A-25 require reimbursement to VA by the NIH for some of the indirect costs of conducting NIH grants at VA facilities. A flat, national rate of reimbursement at 15 percent results in a far lower cost to NIH than the facilities and administration (F&A) rates negotiated with most universities and nonprofit organizations. Further, this lower rate reflects the significant contribution VA will continue to make toward supporting NIH research conducted in its facilities.

The VA/NIH partnership has been greatly strengthened in recent years to our mutual benefit. However, VA cannot continue to support all the F&A costs associated with the increasing amount of NIH-sponsored, university-administered research conducted in VA facilities. At a meeting with VHA representatives held January 19, 2001, Dr. Baldwin indicated the change would be implemented at the beginning of FY 2002. I would appreciate confirmation that the necessary NIH policy change remains on track for implementation.

Page 2.

Ruth Kirschstein, M.D.

I welcome a fair and equitable agreement between VA and NIH, but I am concerned that movement toward a positive resolution appears to have stalled. I hope you will let me know if my staff or I can do anything to maintain momentum on this issue.

Thank you for your consideration and I look forward to your response.

Sincerely,

Thomas L. Garthwaite, M.D.
Under Secretary for Health

cc:
Wendy Baldwin, Ph.D., Deputy Director for Extramural Research, NIH
Joe Cook, Director, Office of Audit Resolution and Cost Policy, DHHS
Carol Tippery, Acting Director, OPERA, NIH
Jordan J. Cohen, M.D., President American Association of Medical Colleges
Barbara West, Executive Director, NAVREF

Mr. BOOZMAN. Ms. Berkley?

Ms. BERKLEY. I have no questions.

Mr. BOOZMAN. Thank you.

Ms. BERKLEY. Thank you very much.

Mr. BOOZMAN. I'd also like to thank the witnesses again for coming, again, in some cases, for extended distances.

Chairman Moran anticipates moving this legislation, assuming our members agree, at next week's scheduled business meeting of the subcommittee.

While the subcommittee appreciates the VA's view that most capital project decision making should be reserved until the CARES process is completed for each one of them, I don't believe this is going to be the decision of Congress.

Veterans deserve safe, efficient, and updated health care facilities. The CARES process is taking years, and it's difficult for me to believe that the projects we would authorize by passing this bill would be affected by CARES.

So the subcommittee plans to proceed in a regular order. Our objective is to get these projects authorized and gain VA resources, what it needs to commence, as soon as possible.

So thank you very much.

Chairman Moran, do you have anything?

Mr. MORAN. I take it that you're in the concluding moments of this hearing, and I thank the witnesses.

Mr. BOOZMAN. We're in the last moment.

Mr. MORAN. Well, I'll try to leave it in the last moments, and not extend it any longer, but I also wanted to thank you, Mr. Boozman, for filling in in my absence. I've been working on a farm bill conference, and I'm only curious to know if you got along better with the ranking member than I have.

Mr. BOOZMAN. In fact, I really appreciate his patience in dealing with me.

Mr. MORAN. Thank you.

I thank both the ranking member and Mr. Boozman for conducting today's hearing. Thank you.

Mr. BOOZMAN. We're adjourned.

[Whereupon, at 4:25 p.m., the subcommittee was adjourned.]

APPENDIX

Statement of
Honorable Bob Filner
Ranking Member
Subcommittee on Health
Committee on Veterans Affairs
April 24, 2002

Legislative Hearing on H.R. 4514
Veterans' Major Medical Facilities Construction Act of 2002

Good afternoon, Mr. Chairman. VA's health care infrastructure has suffered the sad consequences of gross under-funding for at least a decade now. I am pleased to be a co-sponsor of this bill to authorize and appropriate VA with a much-needed infusion of funds for major construction projects.

While some VA facilities are relatively new, we know that the average age of most facilities is 50 years (half of a century old!) Aging infrastructures, like aging bodies, need more than a band-aid and an aspirin! I believe Congress has an obligation to help VA maintain a safe and decent health care system for our nation's veterans. And I look forward to taking action to begin the process of addressing these shortfalls of the past.

Thank you to the witnesses who have traveled from the far corners of the country to be with us today. A special welcome to Gary Rossio, Chief Executive Officer of the VA San Diego Healthcare System.

This bill, H.R. 4514, authorizes the Secretary to carry out ten major medical construction projects and appropriates $285 million to fund these same projects. The bill is fiscally responsible. I applaud and support that feature. The bill is also responsive to addressing my concerns and the concerns of this Committee for the safety of VA patients and employees. I cannot emphasize enough: seismic corrections are an urgent need in my home State of California, and I am encouraged to see that six of the ten major construction projects are committed to fixing the structural integrity of some of the most at-risk facilities in VA's system.

We're also raising the threshold for major construction projects to those that cost more than $6 million. This facet of the bill gives the Secretary more flexibility and keeps pace with the rising costs in the construction industry across the country.

These provisions will help to nurture and revitalize the desolate situation we've created with the inactions of the past.

Thank you.

Prepared statement of Congressman Brown

VA Health Subcommittee Hearing,
April 24, 2002, 3:00 p.m., 334 Cannon HOB

Mr. Chairman, thank you for holding this Subcommittee Hearing today. Like most members of this committee, I am very concerned about the conditions of many of our VA medical facilities. I was very disappointed when the Senate did not take action after the House passed H.R. 811, the Veterans Hospital Emergency Repair Act, last year. I know that many are frustrated with the VA's Capital Asset Realignment or CARES process that seems to have no end in sight.

I want to commend the Chairman for pushing for nearly $285 million in VA major medical facilities construction in this bill. However, I am a little concerned that most of this funding is dedicated to projects in California to make seismic improvements to various buildings. Are we putting all of our eggs in one basket? I think we need to be very careful to ensure that we take a broad look at all facilities throughout the country before we make final decisions on these projects. We should also not forget about the funding that is still required at all VA medical facilities to cover maintenance and repair work on the current infrastructure that is already in place.

The Ralph H. Johnson VA Medical Center, located in Charleston, South Carolina, offers all levels of inpatient and outpatient care thanks in great part to its successful affiliation with the Medical University of South Carolina. However, this facility was constructed in 1966, and like the Naval Hospital located nearby, is outmoded for delivering health care in a modern and efficient manner. Here is just one example where VA could work to build a state-of-the-art facility for our veterans even in coordination with the Defense Department.

Mr. Chairman, thanks again for holding this hearing today and thank you to all of the witnesses for their testimony.

VA Health Subcommittee Hearing,
April 24, 2002, 3:00 p.m., 334 Cannon HOB

Potential Hearing Questions:

For Panel 1, VA:

1. Of the 10 major medical facility construction projects listed in Section 2 of H.R. 4514, 6 involve seismic corrections at VA buildings in the state of California at a cost of more than $160 million? It seems like most of the rest of the country is getting shut out in this bill. Why has the VA chosen to focus upon these facilities as their priorities? Is the risk of damage from seismic disturbances so great that all of our resources should be dedicated in this area?

2. What is the long-range plan for building new facilities where VA and DoD medical care can be co-located so that beneficiaries receive quality care in a seamless environment? In Charleston, we have a 1974 Naval Hospital and a 1966 VA Medical Facility that are outmoded for delivering health care in an efficient and modern manner. There are other buildings in a similar state throughout the nation. Will the CARES program, with its potential realignment of VA capital assets, help make some of these projects a reality?

3. Besides major medical facilities construction, there is also concern that we are not providing enough funding to adequately cover the maintenance and repair work on the existing infrastructure. I have heard that there exists deficits of millions of dollars within some networks. Will VA officials have to transfer a portion of their operating budget to cover maintenance and repair work at their facilities? If so, how can this be done without impacting the quality of care or personnel levels?

PREPARED OPENING STATEMENT OF CONGRESSWOMAN BERKLEY

- Thank you, Mr. Chairman.
- I know that this bill authorizes necessary construction projects for veterans' medical facilities across the country. Veterans everywhere deserve the highest quality health care possible and that requires the highest quality health care facilities. This legislation is a step in that direction.
- However, I would be remiss if I did not take this opportunity to remind the committee, as I have so many times, of similar needs in my own district.
- Everyone here knows of the large and growing veterans population in southern Nevada. Good health care is so important to them and, unfortunately, often too hard to obtain.
- Recently, the ambulatory care clinic in Las Vegas sustained severe structural damage. This clinic is one of the *primary* sources of health care for veterans in my district, and it will have to be evacuated and shut down while repairs, if repairs are possible, are being made.
- Although the VA is working hard to ensure that medical care for southern Nevada veterans is not disrupted during these repairs, I believe this is an ideal. opportunity to reevaluate the veterans health care facilities that exist in my district.
- The ambulatory care clinic in Las Vegas will face a nearly 100 percent increase in their case load during the next eight years. Veterans in southern Nevada need a bigger, more comprehensive facility to meet their needs, and I believe a full service VA hospital is the only answer.
- As the committee considers this legislation and others like it, I will continue to talk about the needs in my district. I look forward to working with this committee and the veterans administration to provide the best health care possible to southern Nevada veterans.
- Thank you.

Statement of Representative Jeff Miller
House Veterans Affairs Committee
Hearing on H.R. 4514, the Veterans' Major Medical Facilities
Construction Act of 2002
April 24, 2002

Thank you Mr. Chairman.

I would like to thank the members of our panels present today. I appreciate your testimony and your assistance with this issue.

H.R. 4514, the Veterans' Major Medical Facilities Construction Act of 2002, would authorize the Secretary to undergo 10 major construction projects in the upcoming fiscal year; increase the threshold for major facility construction projects; and would adjust the criteria for the Secretary's selection of minor projects for funding.

It is of the utmost importance that this Committee not only exercise its oversight role, but also its role and responsibility in guiding capital investment within the VA Healthcare System. On this Committee we tend to focus on access and quality of the care, and we must ensure that a safe, viable infrastructure is there to provide it.

Glaringly absent from the VA's Construction Programs Budget Request was funding for a medical center or an additional outpatient clinic in Northwest Florida. As I have stated before, Northwest Florida is home to nearly 109,000 veterans, yet there is not a single in-patient bed available to them. Additionally, our two outpatient clinics in Pensacola

and Panama City are strained to the point where veterans are forced to wait months on end for an appointment.

That having been said, I know that all of us in this room are dedicated to providing all that we can for our nation's finest, and I would hope that additional infrastructure to service the large population down in my district would be in the Administration's future plans. Deputy Assistant Secretary Catlett and Mr. Yarborough, I look forward to working with you in the coming months on this issue and would like to extend an invitation to you to visit the Emerald Coast to witness our need firsthand.

I would like to thank Chairman Moran for calling this hearing today to discuss this important issue. I am pleased that the Committee is fulfilling its obligation to oversee and help guide VA capital investment, and I hope that this year our counterparts on the Senate side do the same. I look forward to the testimony.

Statement of

Mark Catlett

Principal Deputy Assistant Secretary for Management

Department of Veterans Affairs

Before the

Subcommittee on Health

House Veterans' Affairs Committee

April 24, 2002

Good afternoon Mr. Chairman. I am pleased to testify today on behalf of the Department of Veterans Affairs (VA) regarding H.R. 4514 entitled, the "Veterans' Major Medical Facilities Construction Act of 2002", authorizing the Secretary of Veterans Affairs to carry out certain major medical construction projects, as well as addressing other matters related to VA's Construction program.

Mr. Chairman, my comments regarding this bill will pertain to the four substantive sections individually, rather than the bill as a whole. With that in mind, let me turn to Section 2, entitled, "Authorization of Major Medical Facility Projects".

Section 2. Authorization of Major Medical Facility Projects

Section 2 of H.R. 4514 would authorize the Secretary to carry out the following ten major medical construction projects:

- Seismic corrections on Building No. 2 at the VA Medical Center in Palo Alto, California in the amount of $14,020,000;
- Seismic corrections on Building No. 4 at the VA Medical Center in Palo Alto, California in the amount of $21,750,000;
- Seismic corrections at the VA Medical Center in San Francisco, California, in the amount of $31,000,000;
- Seismic corrections at the VA Medical Center in West Los Angeles, California, in the amount of $27,200,000;
- Seismic corrections and clinical improvements at the VA Medical Center in Long Beach, California, in the amount of $24,600,000;

- Seismic corrections on Building No. 1 at the VA Medical Center in San Diego, California, in the amount of $47,100,000;
- Construction involving the consolidation of the Ambulatory Surgery and Clinical Care facilities at the VA Medical Center in Cleveland, Ohio, in the amount of $32,500,000;
- Construction involving the consolidation of VA and DoD health and benefits offices in Anchorage, Alaska, in the amount of $59,000,000;
- Construction involving the renovation of certain wards at the VA Medical Center in West Haven, Connecticut, in the amount of $15,300,000; and,
- Construction involving the expansion of the Ambulatory Care facility at the VA Medical Center in Tampa, Florida, in the amount of $12,400,000.

The first four projects in the bill were also included in the President's FY 2003 budget submission to Congress. The selection of these projects was the result of a thorough capital investment selection process in which specific needs of VA were balanced against the Department's strategic goals, within the parameters of annual budget constraints. The ultimate result of this process was the selection of four major construction projects that VA believes best achieve this balance and that reflect a sound financial investment. Moreover, the projects selected by the Department are the least likely to be affected by the ongoing CARES process. As you know, the CARES process has been implemented to improve access and quality of veterans' health care through realigning VA's capital assets. CARES is an objective evidence-based evaluation of clinical services required in the year 2020, by market area. We believe it is premature at this time to recommend additional projects.

While I am addressing the projects included in H.R. 4514, I would like to mention that our FY 2003 budget requested authorization for the lease of a satellite outpatient clinic in Charlotte, North Carolina, in the amount of $2,626,000. We would ask that this authorization be included in the bill when it is marked up.

Section 3. Authorization of Appropriations

Section 3 of the bill authorizes for appropriation the sum of $285,000,000 for FY 2003 for construction of the ten major medical projects listed in Section 2.

My comment on Section 3 is consistent with my previous comments regarding Section 2. Specifically, since it is VA's determination that only the four projects listed in the President's FY 2003 Budget submission to Congress should be carried out at this time, the amount authorized to be appropriated for fiscal year 2003 for major construction projects should be $93,970,000 for seismic corrections on Buildings No. 2 ($14,020,000) and No. 4 ($21,750,000) at the VA Medical Center in Palo Alto, California; seismic corrections at the VA Medical Center in San Francisco, California ($31,000,000); and, Seismic corrections at the VA Medical Center in West Los Angeles, California ($27,200,000).

The physical infrastructure of the VA health care system is one of the largest in the Federal government. While some VA facilities are relatively new, the average age of VA buildings is 50 years. During the past few years, there has been a reluctance to commit to capital investment out of concern that VA was unsure of facilities that would clearly be needed in the future. As we complete our CARES initiatives that identify options to improve our health care system and provide better access, infrastructure modifications will create a large number of projects for future funding and authorization.

Section 4. Increase in Threshold for Major Medical Facility Construction Projects

Section 4 of H.R. 4514 is entitled Increase in Threshold for Major Medical Facility Construction Projects. Subsection (a) of Section 4 increases the dollar threshold that defines a major construction project from its current dollar amount of more than $4,000,000 to more than $6,000,000. Subsection (b) of Section 4 seeks to identify those projects to which the increased threshold applies. VA is currently reviewing Section 4 of the bill and we will provide the Committee with our views on this provision at a later time.

Section 5. Criteria for Minor Construction Projects

Section 5 of H.R. 4514 is entitled Criteria For Minor Construction Projects. The language of this section directs the Secretary to select minor construction projects to improve, replace, renovate, or update facilities to achieve improvements in one or more of five specific areas. While this language may have been included to provide guidance to VA in prioritizing the Department's minor construction projects, it eliminates the discretion that the Secretary now has in identifying those minor construction projects that will best meet the overall needs of the Department. VA's comprehensive process for selecting the minor construction projects that will best fulfill VA's mission makes Section 5 of the bill unnecessary. Accordingly, I strongly recommend that it be removed from H.R. 4514.

This concludes my formal testimony.

DEPARTMENT OF THE AIR FORCE

PRESENTATION TO THE

COMMITTEE ON VETERANS' AFFAIRS

SUBCOMMITTEE ON HEALTH

COMMITTEE ON GOVERNMENT REFORM

UNITED STATES HOUSE OF REPESENTATIVES

SUBJECT: VETERANS' MAJOR MEDICAL FACILITIES CONSTRUCTION ACT OF 2002

STATEMENT OF: COLONEL DAVID D. GILBREATH COMMANDER, ELMENDORF AFB HOSPITAL

24 APRIL 2002

Mister Chairman and distinguished members of the committee:

It is an honor to have the opportunity to discuss with you today how the 3rd Medical Group is working with the Alaska VA Healthcare System to provide comprehensive, quality healthcare to the veterans of Alaska. My comments today will include a brief history of our DoD/VA Joint Venture, a description of how it now works and finally a discussion of the opportunities for further integration of services provided by the proposed new VA clinic adjacent to the 3rd Medical Group hospital.

Overview and History

Alaska's immense size, intimidating terrain, distance from the Continental United States, and high cost of living, present a variety of challenges to delivering health care to the more than 100,000 Department of Defense and Veterans Affairs beneficiaries who live in Alaska. Alaska is a huge state, with a land mass one-fifth the size of the Continental United States. Road systems in Alaska are sparse. There is only one two-lane road that connects the state's two largest cities of Anchorage and Fairbanks. This, coupled with the severe weather conditions, make land travel difficult at best. Alaska is sparsely populated. The state averages less than one person per square mile compared to 70 people per square mile for the Continental United States. Nearly 25% of Alaskans live in towns or villages that can only be reached by plane or boat. Twenty five percent of Alaskans live in communities with fewer than 1,000 people. The vast majority of the state's physicians reside in the Anchorage area, which has nearly half of the state's population of approximately 650,000. Many Alaskan communities are medically underserved. For example, hundreds of small villages scattered around the state rely on health aides with an 8th grade education as their sole source of day-to-day medical care. Incredibly, outside Anchorage, there isn't a single practicing cardiologist any where in the state. All these factors contribute to the high cost of health care in Alaska and add to the complexities of providing health care to VA and DoD beneficiaries in this environment.

The VA has never had an inpatient medical facility in Alaska. They have always purchased inpatient services from the private sector. In 1986, an economic analysis by the Army Corps of Engineers, concluded that a cost-effective health care delivery alternative for veterans in the Anchorage area, was a DoD/VA joint venture with the Air Force at Elmendorf Air Force Base. The VA contributed $11.2M towards construction of a $164M 110-bed, 450,000 square foot, medical facility on Elmendorf AFB. Construction began in 1993 and the birth of the Elmendorf DoD/VA Joint Venture occurred in May 1999, when the 3rd Medical Group cut the ribbon on its new medical facility.

Principles of Operation of the Current Joint Venture

Ours is one of eight DoD/VA joint ventures and has been the focus of national attention since its inception. It was called a "model for the rest of the country" by VA Secretary Principi, during a visit to Alaska last year. The Joint Venture's principles of operation call for an integrated, jointly staffed medical facility to meet the health care needs of DoD and VA beneficiaries. The VA staffs the Intensive Care Unit and the Air Force staffs the Medical Surgical Unit. Since February 1, 2000, the VA also provides staffing to augment our emergency room. On that date, the Joint Venture became the ER of choice for Anchorage veterans. This has been a huge success because historical data showed that over 25 percent of ER visits by veterans in Anchorage hospitals resulted in an admission. Veterans requiring admission from the ER are now admitted to the Joint Venture hospital, rather than costly hospitals in the private sector.

The Air Force runs the hospital on a day-to-day basis with input from the VA on various committees. The VA reimburses the AF for services provided on a per diem basis for inpatient care and on a fee-schedule basis for outpatient visits and ancillary services. Currently, the VA employs approximately 50 staff members at the Joint Venture, compared to approximately 800 staff and another 150 contractors provided by the Air Force.

A major goal of the Joint Venture is to increase access to medical care for veterans, while containing costs. During FY01, over 700 veterans were admitted to the Joint Venture hospital, a 24 percent increase from the previous year. During that same period, emergency room visits increased 19 percent to nearly 2,000 patients. Because of differing accounting systems, it is difficult to compute exact cost avoidance savings.

The Elmendorf Joint Venture strives to make a seamless continuum of inpatient care, as well as selected outpatient care, available to Alaska's veterans, while enhancing the range of services available to DoD beneficiaries. The joint venture is designed to improve the healthcare delivery system for all eligible federal beneficiaries. It offers VA beneficiaries a local, federal inpatient facility while DoD beneficiaries enjoy expanded access to specialty care, including the ICU and cardiology services provided by the VA.

Special emphasis has been put into place to ensure one standard of care for all patients receiving treatment in the Joint Venture. Staff from both agencies work hard to overcome cultural and mission differences to ensure we meet the common goal to: "Take care of the men and women who have served and continue to serve this great nation." During our March 2002, Joint Commission on Accreditation of Healthcare Organizations visit, surveyors praised the Joint Venture for its cost effectiveness and adherence to one standard of care.

Opportunities for Further Integration with Proposed Clinic

The VA's proposed clinic adjacent to the 3rd Medical Group offers significant opportunities for further integration of services that currently are not feasible because of geographical separation between the AF hospital and the existing VA outpatient clinic. To date, we have held nine meetings between the staff of the 3rd Medical Group and staff of the Alaska VA Healthcare System to identify sharing opportunities and ways to reduce the square footage requirement of the proposed VA clinic. Preliminary results are very encouraging. Many areas have been identified as having excess capacity for sharing with the VA. So far, our warehouse, radiology, medical laboratory, central sterile supply, and medical library have been identified as having the most potential for integration. Sharing in these areas should significantly reduce the need for these services in the new VA clinic, thereby producing significant savings in the final scope of the project. Also, building a VA outpatient clinic adjacent to the 3rd Medical Group offers some cost-effective economies of scale through joint housekeeping contracts, shared maintenance contracts and so on. Also, an adjacent clinic would present opportunities to share our in-house biomedical equipment repair service with the VA.

It should be pointed out that a huge factor that inhibits more complete integration is incompatible information management systems between the two agencies. It has been frequently identified that the lack of compatibility between the VA clinical information system and DoD's Composite Health Care System (CHCS) provides a huge roadblock in efficiently integrating operations. In many cases, such duplication often causes redundant data entry and wasted man-hours. For example, because of incompatible information systems, near-term integration of Pharmacy Services appears impractical until information technology solutions are developed. However, the DoD and VA are actively working to improve information sharing between medical data systems.

I am confident that construction of a new VA clinic within the immediate proximity of the 3rd Medical Group will further improve our abilities to share resources and services. Land is available for construction and our current facility has enough excess utility capability to supply this new building. While concerns over security and access have increased since September 11, 2001, recent meetings with Air Force Security Forces personnel have helped devise a plan where access to healthcare for Veterans is ensured while also maintaining the security posture essential to protecting the critical national security assets based on Elmendorf Air Force Base.

Conclusion

I believe that a new VA clinic built adjacent to the 3rd Medical Group will dramatically improve access to timely, cost-effective, quality health care services to veterans in Alaska. The men and women of the 3rd Medical Group look forward to working with the VA to make this happen. This will definitely be a win for the VA, a win for the DoD and a huge win for the American taxpayer!

Mister Chairman and distinguished members of this committee, thank you for this opportunity to report on the challenges and successes of the Alaska DoD/VA Joint Venture and thank you for your continued advocacy and support of our nation's veterans.

FOVA

Friends of VA Medical Care and Health Research

A coalition of national organizations committed to quality care for America's veterans

Executive Committee

Charles Clayton
Association of
Professors of Medicine
202-861-7700

Gary Ewart
American Thoracic Society
202-785-3355

Jonathan Fishburn
Association of
American Medical Colleges
202-828-0526

Larry Soler
Juvenile Diabetes Foundation
International
202-371-9746

Lynn Morrison
American Federation for
Medical Research
202-543-7460

Barbara West
National Association of
Veterans' Research and
Education Foundations
301-229-1048

Testimony

Presented Before the

Committee on Veterans Affairs

Subcommittee on Health

Regarding

The Need for a Dedicated Funding Stream for Research Facility Improvements

Presented by

Antonio Laracuente

Chairman

National Association of Veterans' Research and Education Foundations (NAVREF)

On Behalf of the

Friends of VA Medical Care and Health Research (FOVA)

April 24, 2002

- On the West Coast, a VA researcher was funded for a project that requires storing tissue samples in sub-zero freezers. The grant supports the purchase of the freezers and space has been allocated. However, the VA facility is unable to fund the $30,000 cost of the necessary electrical upgrade.
- At several VA facilities, the air vent intakes for the research floors are directly over the hospital loading dock and in certain conditions, they draw exhaust and garbage fumes into the laboratories. No funding is available to relocate the intakes or install air locks.
- At another facility, window air conditioning units are inadequate. During the summer, investigators and their technicians work late at night, the only time the labs are cool enough that the petri dish gels won't melt. Tests frequently have to be repeated due to the high temperatures. No funding is available to install a central air conditioning system.
- The animal laboratory at another West Coast facility is located one floor above patient care areas. Water from cage washing was found to be leaking down into the clinical spaces. As a result, the animal facility can use only one room, a space that is inadequate for the researchers' needs. Funding is needed to build a new animal facility located away from patient care areas.

I have more examples of research facility problems to discuss, but first, thank you, Mr. Chairman and members of this Subcommittee for the opportunity to present testimony. I am Antonio Laracuente, executive director of the Atlanta Research and Education Foundation, and I am here today as chairman of the National Association of Veterans' Research and Education Foundations (NAVREF) on behalf of the Friends of VA Medical Care and Health Research (FOVA).

We applaud this Subcommittee for its leadership in securing House passage of H.R. 811, the *Veterans Hospital Emergency Repair Act*, and for incorporating in that bill an allocation to upgrade and renovate VA's research facilities. I think we both share much regret that the appropriation died in conference. The bill came close to accomplishing what I am here to ask for today – a dedicated funding stream for renovation and repair of VA's existing research facilities. Major construction of new research facilities is an important topic and as far as we can determine, in recent years not a single major construction research project has been proposed by VA — or authorized much less funded — to replace the inadequate World War II era buildings that house much of the VA research program. However, in my testimony, I will focus on less costly, but equally important, needs.

The VA research program is of consistently high quality and remarkably productive. Despite shortcomings in the research facilities, every week the press reports medical breakthroughs by VA researchers that make a positive impact on the health of every American. VA researchers regularly win national recognition awards and publish their results in the most stringently reviewed medical journals. Conditions in the facilities are difficult, but the safety of VA patients and staff are paramount. However, I believe VA is reaching the point where a significant investment in the research infrastructure is essential.

In our opinion, the current practice of allocating all minor construction funding to one appropriation no longer serves VA facilities well. Congress has mandated that VA provide care and conduct research, yet construction funding for both is provided in one appropriation that is distributed largely on the basis of clinical relevance at both the Central Office and VISN levels. Research cannot — and we feel should not — compete with medical center needs for new elevators, heating systems, or renovations in patient areas. Nor should research needs be met at the expense of clinical needs. In recent years, the minor construction appropriation has been chronically inadequate to meet even high priority clinical needs so little, if anything, is "left over" for research.

Network and medical center directors make an effort to search out funding for research facilities, cutting a little here and there and in some cases, relying on the affiliated universities and research foundations to contribute to the most basic, necessary renovations. In the last year alone, thanks to VISN funding, one facility had a back up electrical system and sprinklers installed at a cost of $600,000. Still awaiting funding are plans for upgrading the elevators and expanding the biosafety laboratories. However, funding for these long overdue renovations is the exception, not the rule. The medical care appropriation is severely strained, the affiliates have their own funding priorities, and few of the research corporations have the resources to fill in the gaps. When money can be scraped together, all too often the amount is inadequate to meet facility-wide needs, such as a new venting and air conditioning system for the animal facility, or project-specific needs such as upgrading a lab to biosafety level three which is essential for the hepatitis C and HIV research projects so relevant to our veteran patients. An investigator gets a grant and then the scramble begins to find the money to upgrade the plumbing, install a hood or move a wall. In my opinion, the lack of a systematic approach to funding these needs is unacceptable for a world-class research program.

VA's research laboratories are falling into disrepair and are increasingly unable to accommodate modern science. Many appear to be on the brink of jeopardizing patient, staff and even animal safety.

- When an animal facility is too small, investigators bring the animals into their regular laboratories, exposing themselves and staff to occupational illnesses. OSHA inspectors have expressed concerns and in one case, said that if it were up to OSHA, the building would be shut down.
- During an annual inspection, a Fire Marshall recommended that research laboratories no longer be housed in one building because the building lacks fire sensors and a sprinkler system.
- Back up generators are needed to ensure safe temperatures in animal facilities on hot days.
- During a hazardous materials drill last December, a local fire department spread banana oil to mimic a toxic spill. Within 15 minutes, oil applied on the 4th floor of the research building was identified on the 2nd and 4th floors of the adjoining patient care facility.

VA research personnel are extremely creative problem solvers, but we are using band-aid solutions. I believe VA is reaching a crisis point at many facilities across the country.

As Dr. Wilson will discuss in a moment, the state of VA's research facilities makes VA a less attractive research partner for NIH and the affiliated universities, reducing investigators' ability to leverage VA funding with other federal and private sector grants. Less than state-of-the-art research facilities also impact medical centers' ability to attract investigators to VA, particularly clinician investigators, those who have the most direct impact on the quality of care provided to veterans. In Atlanta, candidates are generally satisfied with the salaries VA offers if laboratories that meet their needs can be provided. Too often, we cannot provide that guaranty. Sometimes we try to find suitable space at the University, but if we are successful, the researchers have to spend time traveling back and forth, are separated from their VA colleagues and are less accessible to their veteran patients.

Thanks in large part to this Subcommittee, the VA research appropriation has grown and we hope it will continue to do so in FY 2003 and beyond. Concurrently, VA investigators are remarkably successful in competing for NIH and other federal awards as well as private sector grants. However, expansion of VA's research facilities has not kept pace with the increase in the number of projects conducted by VA investigators. This has created an urgent need for new research space. In some cases, a new building is warranted. In others, conversion of former wards into research laboratories is a better solution, but funding is unavailable.

I suspect that every research office across the nation maintains a list of urgently needed repairs, improvements and expansion needs. Unfortunately, at most facilities, the lists get longer each year, not shorter. To address this tremendous backlog and establish reliable resources in the future, Friends of VA urges this Subcommittee to establish a funding stream specifically for research facility improvements. This would recognize that both research and medical care have essential, but often distinct and differing, construction needs. We recommend central management of the funds by the Office of Research and Development (ORD) so the most pressing needs can be prioritized among large and small upgrades as well as facility-wide and project-specific needs. It is important to recognize that ORD is conducting ongoing site visits to review and inventory the specific research facility infrastructure at every VA medical center. As a result, ORD has the data necessary to prioritize the need for improvements nationwide.

As well as a list showing research facilities in need of major construction funding, the VA has a list of 15 priority sites in need of significant renovation with price tags ranging from $1 million to nearly $4 million. Some involve replacing inadequate buildings while others provide for renovation of existing space. These add up to $42 million, close to the Friends of VA recommendation of $45 million. FOVA would like to see the additional $3 million reserved for smaller, project-specific needs.

Taking off my Friends of VA hat for a moment, I would like to briefly mention that a partial solution to the problem of funding for VA's research facilities exists in what we call the "15% VA- add on." As you may be aware, when a VA researcher's NIH grant is administered by the affiliated university, but the work is conducted in a VA laboratory, NIH provides the university with administration funds only. NIH provides nothing to support the VA's cost of providing facilities in which to conduct the work. NAVREF has long maintained that NIH should pay its fair share of VA's costs by adding 15% to the university's administrative overhead rate, or to the rate of any other VA-affiliated institution that administers NIH grants for VA investigators working in VA facilities. This amount should then be passed through to VA medical centers to support their facilities costs. Last year, VA investigators received NIH grants totaling about $350 million. VA has calculated that typically 44% of NIH awards to VA investigators are conducted in university facilities and presumably qualify for the university's on-campus facilities and administration (F&A) rate. If applied to the 56% conducted in VA facilities, the 15% VA-add on rate would have generated a cash flow of nearly $30 million last year.

It is our understanding that only a Department of Health and Human Services policy change is needed to implement the VA-add on, but for six years, VA and NIH have failed to reach an agreement on this issue. I respectfully ask you to work with your colleagues on the Energy and Commerce Committee to advance this matter to a favorable solution. The R&D appropriation supports about half of the VA research portfolio and we feel VA's research partners — universities, NIH, the research corporations and others — should share the facilities costs to ensure that VA laboratories meet the highest standards of safety and are capable of supporting cutting edge research.

But the 15% VA-add on is far from the full solution. We urge this Subcommittee to authorize a centrally administered, dedicated funding stream specifically for improvements in VA's research facilities. We sincerely appreciate that research is incorporated in the *Veterans Major Medical Facilities Construction Act of 2002*, but we are concerned that research needs may be relegated to the bottom of the priority list and will remain unfunded. In our view, research facilities should be on a **separate** priority list with explicitly designated funding.

Finally, on April 16, your Senate counterparts introduced S. 2132, the *Medical Research Enhancement Act of 2002* which follows the lead of this Subcommittee on establishing VA medical emergency preparedness and research centers. We strongly support both bills, but wish to note that the Senate has included a few provisions that would allow the nonprofit research and education corporations to better serve their medical centers. I ask for your support of these provisions in conference.

Thank you for your consideration. I would be pleased to answer your questions.

Statement

Of the

Association of American Medical Colleges

On

Veterans Major Medical Facilities Construction

Presented to the

Subcommittee on Health
Committee on Veterans' Affairs
United States House of Representatives

By

Donald E. Wilson, M.D.
Vice President for Medical Affairs and Dean
University of Maryland School of Medicine

April 24, 2002

Good Afternoon Mr. Chairman and Members of the Subcommittee. Thank you for the opportunity to address you on this important issue. I am Donald Wilson, vice president for medical affairs, University of Maryland, and dean of the School of Medicine. Today, I am representing the Association of American Medical Colleges (AAMC). The AAMC represents the nation's 125 accredited allopathic medical schools, over 400 major teaching hospitals and health systems including 72 Veterans Affairs Medical Centers, 98 academic and scientific societies representing 105,000 faculty members and the nation's 66,000 medical student and 97,000 residents. As I am sure you know, 107 of those 125 medical schools maintain formal affiliation agreements with VA medical centers and these agreements are mutually beneficial to both the academic partner and the VA in each of the VA's three major missions of patient care, research and education.

The Subcommittee, I am sure, is familiar with the importance of the affiliation agreements to both the VA and the affiliated health professions schools. The AAMC has testified to this relationship several times over the last few years; however, those statements have most often focused on the education and patient care missions rather than research. From the standpoint of a dean of an affiliated medical school, I see the VA research program as an opportunity for collaboration, as a dedicated funding source that the faculty at my school can access, and as a tool I can use in faculty recruiting. The success rates for VA research grants are greater than those of the NIH and the natural physical proximity of the facilities lends itself to collaborative research efforts.

One of the problems that the research facilities face is the competition in the VA Minor Construction budget account for limited funds. The VA research program has seen some significant increases in recent years, but funds are statutorily prohibited from being used for construction or renovation. Even if they were able to be used, the program is still not big enough to address the critical research needs and the facilities issues. Research facility needs less than $4 million are funded through the Minor Construction line item, competing against other VA facility needs not necessarily related to research such as parking lots, elevators, air conditioners, etc. For this reason the AAMC believes that the research enterprise would be well served if the Subcommittee supported a separate funding stream that would be dedicated to upgrading and improving existing research facilities. From the affiliate standpoint, it would allow an academic institution to count on the VA facility as a potential site for state-of-the-art research. As recommended by the Friends of VA Medical Care and Health Research Coalition, such a line item would fund one-time construction or renovation projects, and be merit-reviewed based on VA's assessment of needs. The Friends of VA have recommended an appropriation of $45 million for this account in the first year.

There are many anecdotal examples of problems with research competing with other needs. One example is the air vent intake at the VA Boston Healthcare System that is located over the hospital loading dock and draws exhaust fumes into the laboratories in certain instances. It would take $300,000 to relocate the intake, but in six successive years, funding has not been available, which limits the potential research that can be conducted in this laboratory by both VA and the affiliated Harvard researchers. Another relates to a researcher who has funding lined up for a grant that requires storing tissue samples in sub-zero freezers, which are covered as a direct cost of the grant. The space has been allocated, but the researcher is unable to secure $30,000 to upgrade the electrical system to support the freezers. VA researchers in Gainesville, Florida are unable to conduct certain types of research because their "wet lab" countertops are made of particle board and formica, rather than the standard stone, and are easily burned and stained from exposure to heat and chemicals. At the Southern Arizona VA Health Care System in Tucson, one of the buildings has no elevator and patients involved in clinical research are required to climb stairs. They also spend precious resources outsourcing kennels for dogs because no funding is available to bring the existing kennels into line with AAALAC or FDA standards.

However, the main reason for my being here this afternoon is not to testify to the poor condition of VA research facilities, but rather to the value of the VA research facilities to the affiliation agreements. One of the obvious benefits is that state-of-the-art research facilities help in the recruitment of top researchers to the affiliated school and therefore, to the faculty of the VA medical center as well. In best case scenarios, top-notch research facilities help both the VA and the affiliate to leverage their research funds. For example, a partnership between the Penn State Milton S. Hershey Medical Center and School of Medicine and the Lebanon, Pennsylvania VA Medical Center recently undertook a joint project to renovate laboratory space at the Lebanon

VA, which will allow researchers with joint appointments to draw down additional federal research dollars from VA and other sources. Under this agreement, the affiliate came up with 75 percent of the needed funds, but without the VA contribution, the project could not have gone forward. As a result, significant research related to regulating blood pressure in cardiac patients, and kidney failure has been able to move forward.

Another good example of the collaboration between affiliates and the VA is at the Texas A&M University System Health Science Center School of Medicine. Several years ago, they began a three way initiative with Scott and White Memorial Hospital and the Central Texas Veterans Health Care System to build a world-class Cardiovascular Research Institute in Temple, Texas. In the true spirit of partnership, these three entities have all contributed significant resources to the initiative, with the university providing the faculty salary lines, the private hospital providing substantial start-up resources, and the VA producing the building. With completion of the building expected this fall, they plan to have three major research groups in Molecular Cardiology, Vascular Biology and Hypertension occupying 35,000 square feet in the building on the VA campus. The interim dean at Texas A&M expects to begin recruiting basic and clinical scientists to the VA within the year. This initiative would not have come about without the full cooperation of the local VA medical center director and the ability to redirect some funds that were targeted for another building. However, the resulting institute provides much greater benefit than any of the partners would have been able to establish on their own.

However, not all the affiliations have such positive stories to tell. At the University of Iowa School of Medicine, about half of the 40,000 square feet of VA research space is located in an aging building that was originally constructed in the 1950s and converted to research space in the 1970s. The HVAC system is so outdated that the labs still use window air conditioners and steam radiators. Researchers are forced to work at night during summer months to avoid melting some of their lab gels and triggering heat shocks to some of their cell lines. The building has no fire sprinkler system or sensors and the Fire Marshall has recommended that the building be discontinued as a research laboratory. As if that wasn't enough, the building has no elevators and large equipment must be fork lifted or craned into the second floor. And due to the age of the building, it can only handle 200 pounds per square foot instead of the standard 600 pounds, limiting the types of instrumentation that can be brought in. All of these issues are unfortunate, but what is perhaps the most disappointing issue at the Iowa VA medical center is that the university feels it cannot in good conscience ask students or postdocs to join these labs. As a result, the university has chosen not to respond to specific program announcements from VA. By undermining the ability of individuals and institutions to leverage additional support from VA and other sources, the quality of science being conducted in the labs is being compromised. Although this extreme example may need major rather than minor construction funds to remedy the problems, the resulting decision to not pursue research funding due directly to the deteriorated state of the facility is a disturbing conclusion.

Dilapidated research facilities also hinder the recruitment process for faculty at both the VA and the affiliated medical school. The University of California, San Diego and the VA San Diego Healthcare system have been unable to recruit a top Hepatitis C specialist because the research space is lacking. Similarly, the University of Colorado Health Sciences Center and the Denver VA Medical Center have been repeatedly turned down by top cardiologists, pulmonary and gastroenterology physicians who cited poor quality research facilities as a major factor in their decisions. This inability to recruit impacts severely on the quality of care for veterans.

Within my own VA affiliation in Baltimore, we are in drastic need of about 20,000 net square feet just to meet our current research space needs. Even though the existing building was only completed in 1993, it is based on designs that took into account the level of research funding from the late 1970s. Funding had increased more than eightfold by the time construction was completed. This year, the VA Maryland Health Care System (VAMHCS) has been awarded about $12.5 million in VA research funding. Those same principal investigators have obtained additional funds from non-VA sources for a total research enterprise of $33 million. Because of a lack of space, at least 18 of those researchers are being housed in University of Maryland School of Medicine laboratories at the expense of the university. Such relationships are only possible because of the close working relationship between myself and the Baltimore VA medical center leadership.

Because of unique geographic and architectural restrictions on the Baltimore VA medical center, the most viable option is to purchase additional space that could be used jointly by the VAMHCS research program and the University of Maryland School of Medicine. In a VA central office survey, the Baltimore VA medical center ranks second nationally in terms of needed renovation with a price tag of approximately $3.5 million needed to ameliorate the current situation. However, minor construction and renovation projects like this one are forced to compete with some of the clinical needs of the VA health care system. I would not suggest that research facility needs should outweigh the needs of the clinical program, but I would suggest that a better process is needed so research facility needs are not consistently left at the bottom of the list.

The importance of the VA affiliation to the research program is not limited to facility issues. The gerontology division at the University of Maryland School of Medicine is totally housed at the VA, and our new state-of-the-art cardiovascular exercise research facility is housed at the VA even though 85 percent of it was funded by the School of Medicine. The VA will soon have a human performance laboratory to look at things such as gait analysis to help diagnose and treat patients suffering from movement disorders and stroke. Additionally, a significant proportion of the Parkinson's disease and multiple sclerosis research that goes on at the School of Medicine is located at the VA. Again, I cannot stress enough that these types of relationships are mutually beneficial to both the VA and the School of Medicine and that the ultimate benefits go to the patients. But the full impact of the potential of the relationship cannot be realized while the VA research facilities are inadequate. For the affiliation partnership to flourish, resources need to come from both partners. Currently, the biggest need on the VA side is research space and I believe that a dedicated funding source for VA research facilities that does not compete directly with clinical needs is necessary to further our shared goals.

In the first session of the 107th Congress, the House passed legislation (H.R. 811) that would have dedicated funding for VA facility construction, with a portion set aside for urgent research needs. I have also had the opportunity to briefly review H.R. 4514, the "Veterans' Major Medical Facilities Construction Act of 2002." First I would like to commend both this subcommittee and the full House VA committee for their leadership and support on this issue. Second, I would like to urge the Congress as a whole to implement a proposal that would provide a dedicated, peer-reviewed funding stream for VA research facility needs. The AAMC, as a member of the Executive Committee of the Friends of VA Medical Care and Health Research Coalition, has endorsed the approach of a separate appropriations line item that I noted earlier in my statement. Whichever approach the committee chooses to pursue, a new authorization or a new appropriations line item within the existing structure, I urge you to make sure than research is not relegated to the bottom of the pile.

In conclusion, let me state again the mutually beneficial characteristics of the VA academic affiliations. It is well documented that the affiliations improve patient care as well as the education of the next generation of our nation's health care professionals. The value of research to the affiliations, the subject of today's hearing is not as well known. My affiliation is not unique. Many affiliations are marked by departments and divisions that are housed in VA space. Many, if not most, of the VA researchers hold joint faculty appointments at the affiliated medical school. The walls between School of Medicine and VA research projects are often blurred as space, funding, and salary support usually come from multiple sources. In order for these affiliations to work with the highest possible efficiency it is necessary for the facilities in which the research is conducted to be state-of-the-art. At the same time, the patient care strains on the VA medical care budget are well documented. VA research facility needs should not be forced to compete against those clinical needs, but nor can they be ignored.

Thank you again for the opportunity to testify this afternoon.

STATEMENT OF
BRIAN E. LAWRENCE
ASSOCIATE NATIONAL LEGISLATIVE DIRECTOR
OF THE
DISABLED AMERICAN VETERANS
BEFORE THE
COMMITTEE ON VETERANS' AFFAIRS
SUBCOMMITTEE ON HEALTH
UNITED STATES HOUSE OF REPRESENTATIVES
APRIL 24, 2002

Mr. Chairman and Members of the Subcommittee:

On behalf of the more than one million members of the Disabled American Veterans (DAV), I appreciate the opportunity to comment on "The Veterans Major Medical Facilities Construction Act of 2002." This would authorize the Secretary of Veterans Affairs to carry out construction projects for the purpose of improving, renovating, and updating Department of Veterans Affairs (VA) medical centers.

As co-authors of the *Independent Budget* (*IB*), the DAV, along with AMVETS, Paralyzed Veterans of America, and the Veterans of Foreign Wars, recommends that major construction projects be funded to make seismic corrections and environmental improvements.

The DAV is pleased with the language of this bill, which would protect vital medical facilities in areas highly vulnerable to earthquakes. In the event of a catastrophic earthquake, these facilities would hopefully withstand the impact. In addition to protecting patients, VA medical centers would become immeasurably important in providing essential medical care to victims in the highly populated metropolitan areas.

This legislation authorizes approximately $165.6 million for seismic corrections. Though the appropriation is $84 million below the required amount estimated in the *IB*, it is welcomed and appreciated.

Structurally sound, modern facilities are necessary to ensure adequate health care, and expansion of ambulatory services enables VA to serve the growing number of patients seeking treatment. This bill responds to changes in the veteran population by expanding ambulatory services in two VA medical centers and renovating another. Thus, DAV Resolutions 082 and 124 are indirectly met via this bill. Resolutions, adopted by our membership, determine the legislative focus of our organization. It is reassuring to recognize similar mandates in the form of legislation.

This bill changes the definition of minor facility construction by increasing the amount that may be spent on minor projects. Currently, expenditures in excess of $4 million are considered major construction projects. Passage of this legislation would raise the threshold for medical projects to $6 million, which addresses an issue, noted in the *IB*, that the current cap is insufficient to cover needed innovations.

The CARES initiative, as well as realignment and consolidation projects, require extensive construction investments that call for a higher spending cap. Though the $6 million cap is well short of the $16 million recommended in the *IB*, we welcome and are grateful for this positive provision.

The DAV was founded on the principle that our nation's first duty to veterans is the rehabilitation of its wartime disabled. High quality medical care is fundamental in this regard.

Mr. Chairman, thank you for the opportunity to present our views on this bill. The Subcommittee's effort to provide better health services for veterans signifies that their dedicated military service to our country is noted and appreciated. Clearly, the DAV's mission to improve the lives of disabled veterans is shared by the Subcommittee. We appreciate your efforts and look forward to working with you in the future on issues important to disabled veterans.

I will be glad to answer any questions this statement may have inspired.

STATEMENT OF

PAUL A. HAYDEN, DEPUTY DIRECTOR
NATIONAL LEGISLATIVE SERVICE
VETERANS OF FOREIGN WARS OF THE UNITED STATES

BEFORE THE

SUBCOMMITTEE ON HEALTH
COMMITTEE ON VETERANS' AFFAIRS
UNITED STATES HOUSE OF REPRESENTATIVES

WITH RESPECT TO

H.R. 4514
VETERANS' MAJOR MEDICAL FACILITIES CONSTRUCTION ACT OF 2002

WASHINGTON, DC APRIL 24, 2002

MR. CHAIRMAN AND MEMBERS OF THE SUBCOMMITTEE:

On behalf of the 2.7 million members of the Veterans of Foreign Wars of the United States (VFW) and our Ladies Auxiliary, and as the organization who authored this year's *Independent Budget* section on the Department of Veterans Affairs' (VA) construction needs, I would like to thank you for the opportunity to communicate our position on what we believe is an important piece of legislation.

The VFW subscribes to the principle that all veterans should have timely access to quality medical care. In order for VA to accomplish this mission, however, they must be able to properly operate, maintain, and improve their facilities. It is for this reason that we are pleased to support the *Veterans' Major Medical Facilities Construction Act of 2002.*

Section 2 of this legislation would expand the number of major medical facility construction projects that VA could accomplish in fiscal year (FY) 2003. Aside from the 4 seismic projects requested in the President's budget, this legislation would authorize VA to carry out an additional 6 projects ranging in category from patient environment to clinical to ambulatory care. It is our understanding that each one of these projects has been scored and is ranked in the top 15 of VA's priorities for major medical construction projects for FY 2003 and as such enjoys our full support.

At this point, I would be remiss if I did not once again emphasize our concern that one year after experiencing a 6.8 magnitude earthquake, the American Lake VA Medical Center in Washington State has yet to receive funding for structural repairs to its main hospital and nursing home.

Section 3 would authorize $285 million to carry out the projects in Section 2. We support this authorization. It is our view that failure to adequately provide for needed major construction projects means monies allocated for health care ultimately get shifted to cover the construction shortfalls to the great detriment of the veteran. By authorizing additional dollars, this legislation is acknowledging that construction funding must be increased to keep VA's facilities in top-rate condition.

The VFW supports Section 4. This section would increase the threshold for major construction projects from $4 million to $6 million. This would, in turn, raise the cap on what constitutes minor construction from projects costing less than $4 million to projects costing less than $6 million. The VFW notes that this current limitation on minor construction funds often forces network directors to string together a series of minor projects to complete changes that are needed to realign or improve facilities or wait their turn for years to secure congressional approval for major funding. This is highly inefficient and leads to unnecessary delays, facility disruptions, and promotes poor fiscal management practices. It is our position that the major construction threshold should be raised to $16 million to adequately allow network directors the flexibility to design and complete projects without unnecessary delays in order to enhance services sooner. We do consider this section, however, a step in the right direction.

Finally, Section 5 of the bill would create criteria for selecting minor construction projects. The VFW supports the 5 categories and sub-categories within the section. We believe, however, that the Secretary should not be limited in the event that a project merits minor construction yet is not articulated by the bill's language. In other words, the Secretary should retain a certain amount of discretion.

This concludes my testimony and I will be pleased to answer any questions you or the members of the subcommittee may have.

STATEMENT OF THE

RICHARD B. FULLER, NATIONAL LEGISLATIVE DIRECTOR

PARALYZED VETERANS OF AMERICA

FOR THE RECORD OF THE

SUBCOMMITTEE ON HEALTH OF THE

HOUSE COMMITTEE ON VETERANS' AFFAIRS

CONCERNING THE

"VETERANS' MAJOR MEDICAL FACILITIES CONSTRUCTION ACT OF 2000"

APRIL 24, 2002

The Paralyzed Veterans of America (PVA) appreciates the opportunity to express our views on the "Veterans' Major Medical Facilities Construction Act of 2002." PVA supports this measure.

Last year, PVA enthusiastically supported H.R. 811, the "Veterans' Hospital Emergency Repair Act." We testified that:

> A study conducted by Price-Waterhouse in 1998 recommended that in order for the VA to protect its facility assets against deterioration and to maintain an adequate and appropriate level of building services, 2 to 4 percent of the assets' replacement value should be spent each year for facility improvements, and another 2 to 4 percent should be expended for nonrecurring maintenance. The VA's total facility assets are valued at approximately $35 billion. Hence, according to the study, the VA should be spending $700 million to $1.4 billion annually, as well as a similar amount for nonrecurring maintenance.

We also stated that "the physical infrastructure of the VA is indeed facing an emergency. With further inaction, a valuable and irreplaceable national asset will be lost, for without health care buildings you do not have a health care system." We appreciate this Subcommittee's hard work on this important issue.

Again this year, *The Independent Budget* called for an additional $250 million to repair seismic deficiencies in VA buildings. We are pleased that this measure authorizes $285 million for projects in FY 2003, the vast majority involving seismic deficiencies. We also appreciate the Subcommittee's inclusion of raising the $4 million cap on minor construction to $6 million. *The Independent Budget* has recommended that this level be raised to $16 million in order to better finance the scope of many needed construction projects. PVA also applauds the Subcommittee for its explicit recognition of the importance of spinal cord injury centers, specialized services programs, and medical research within the scope of the "Veterans' Major Medical Facilities Construction Act of 2002."

Finally, and perhaps most importantly, PVA wants to state unequivocally that these much needed construction funds must not come at the expense of, or out of the medical care budget line-item that provides direct health care services to veterans. The VA medical system is facing a crisis, a crisis brought about by inadequate funding, a crisis that has lead to health care rationing and shocking waiting times faced by veterans all across this nation. The solution to this crisis lies in providing the funding required by VA health care in the medical care account. The crisis facing VA infrastructure, likewise, will be solved by providing the necessary additional resources in the construction line-item.

PVA wishes to again thank this Subcommittee and offer our support to see the "Veterans' Major Medical Facilities Construction Act of 2002" enacted into law.

**STATEMENT OF
JAMES R. FISCHL, DIRECTOR
NATIONAL VETERANS AFFAIRS AND REHABILITATION COMMISSION
THE AMERICAN LEGION
TO THE
U.S. HOUSE OF REPRESENTATIVES
SUBCOMMITTEE ON HEALTH
COMMITTEE ON VETERANS' AFFAIRS
ON THE
VETERANS' MAJOR MEDICAL FACILITIES ACT OF 2002,
H.R. 4514**

APRIL 24, 2002

Mr. Chairman and Members of the Subcommittee:

The American Legion is pleased to have the opportunity to submit a statement for the record on H.R. 4514, the Veterans' Major Medical Facilities Construction Act of 2002. This Act would authorize the Secretary of Veterans Affairs to carry out several major medical facility projects such as seismic corrections, renovations, and expansions of patient care facilities at Department of Veterans Affairs Medical Centers (VAMCs).

Sec 2. Authorization of Major Medical Facility Projects

This section calls for seismic corrections at Palo Alto, San Francisco, West Los Angeles, Long Beach, and San Diego, California. The American Legion is extremely pleased to see these much needed corrections being addressed. Certainly the past experiences at VAMCs Sepulveda and Palo Alto, CA, where earthquakes compromised buildings and disrupted services, have exemplified the necessity to address seismic issues. The identified construction projects should be a priority because they involve Department of Veterans Affairs (VA) health care facilities located in exceptionally high-risk areas. It is clear that the safety of the patients and the staff is first and foremost in the minds of everyone concerned.

Other proposals under section 2:
(1) Consolidation projects in Cleveland, Ohio and Anchorage, Alaska.
(2) Renovation in West Haven, Connecticut.
(3) Ambulatory Care expansion at VAMC Tampa.

The American Legion's National Field Service had the opportunity to tour the wards at West Haven during a site visit in November 2001. The wards were dated and poorly configured, and they do not meet current expectations or standards for inpatient facilities. VA has well known challenges in aligning and modernizing its capital assets in the face of an expanding workload and an aging infrastructure. These projects will help to address this challenge.

The American Legion supports these proposals.

Sec 3. Authorization of Appropriations.

This provision would authorize appropriations to the Secretary's Construction, Major Projects, account in the amount of $285 million for Fiscal Year (FY) 2003.

On three previous occasions, The American Legion has recommended $310 million for VA Major Construction in FY 2003:

- On September 11, 2001, The American Legion's National Commander, Richard J. Santos, in a written testimony to a joint session of the Veterans' Affairs Committees.
- On February 13, 2002, in written testimony to the President's Budget Request for FY 2003.
- On April 16, 2002, in written testimony to the House Appropriations Subcommittee on VA, HUD, and Independent Agencies.

The American Legion is extremely concerned with the President's proposed VA budget for FY 2003. This includes funding for important major and minor construction projects. It is no secret that VA's construction budget has been miniscule in comparison to its actual needs. For years, the construction budget has suffered to the point that it still falls well short of even the minimum amount needed. VA has not received appropriate funding for Major and Minor Construction projects in years. The American Legion has testified on more than one occasion about the safety issues and concerns dealing with the state of VA buildings. Many more of the buildings within VA, not just the few listed in Section 2 of this Act, are in need of seismic and safety corrections. VA can ill afford to have the lives of patients and employees needlessly placed in danger while being treated at a VAMC.

Simply because the Veterans Health Administration's (VHA) emphasis has shifted from inpatient care to primary care is not a basis to neglect capital assets. The current Capital Assets Realignment for Enhanced Services (CARES) review will potentially determine the future of many VA facilities. However, some projects are too important to postpone. Issues involving patient care, safety, and privacy must not be delayed.

Again, The American Legion recommends $310 million for Major Construction in Section 3 of this Act.

Sec 4. Increase in Threshold for Major Medical Facility Construction Projects.

This section proposes to increase the threshold for major medical facility construction projects from $4,000,000 to $6,000,000.

The American Legion supports this increase.

Sec 5. Criteria for Minor Construction Projects.

This provision would add a new subsection (e) in Section 8103 of title 38, United States Code (USC), which directs the Secretary to select projects to improve, replace, renovate, or update facilities. This new section proposes to list those types of improvements, replacements, renovations and updates the Secretary can achieve. Such things as, seismic protection, fire safety, utility systems and ancillary, patient care facilities improvements are among them.

The American Legion is concerned with the fate of a project if it falls outside of the finite criteria listed under this proposed new section, yet falls within the range for minor construction dollars. There would be no way for the project to get funded under this proposal. The American Legion questions the reason for the list in the first place. The American Legion believes it should be within the Secretary's discretion to decide which Minor Construction projects merit funding, and which are the most urgent.

Conclusion

The American Legion advocates for adequate VA construction appropriations every year. The American Legion's recommendations are based on a sound, realistic assessment of system wide needs. VA has many urgent construction requirements. The American Legion recognizes that this Act is a good first step in the right direction. We also appreciate the fact that it does address one of the biggest safety issues within VA, seismic corrections. However, there is much more to be done.

Mr. Chairman, we applaud you and the distinguished Members of this Subcommittee for the work you have done and that which you continue to do for the Nation's veterans and their families.

APEX
TP
9780160709142
76901945 — 95